PRIMARY MATHEMATICS

WORKBOOK 2B

Common Core Edition

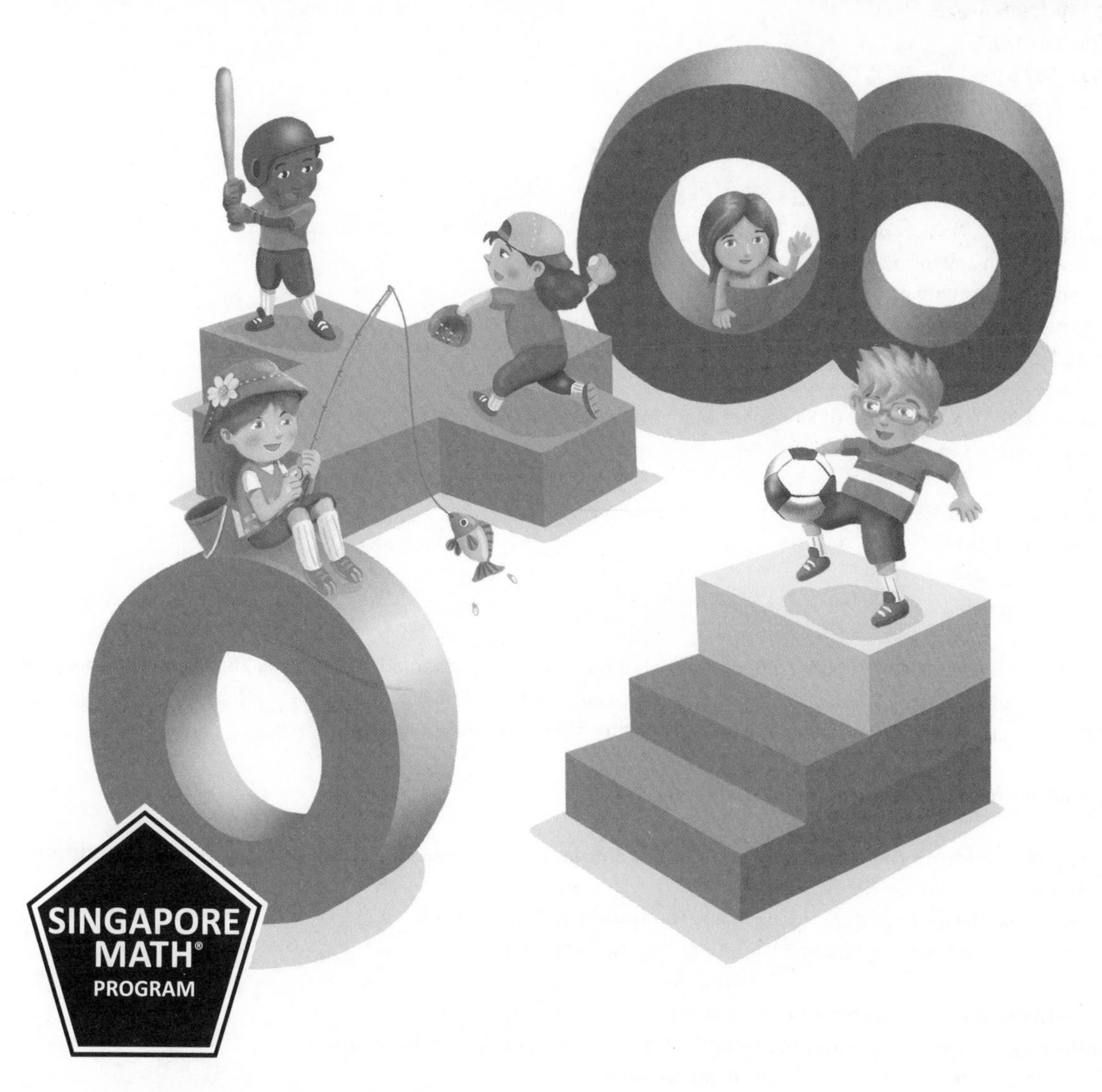

US Distributor

Original edition published under the title Primary Mathematics Workbook 2B

Published by Times Media Private Limited

Published by Marshall Cavendish Education
Times Centre, 1 New Industrial Road, Singapore 536196
Customer Service Hotline: (65) 6213 9444
US Office Tel: (1-914) 332 8888 | Fax: (1-914) 332 8882
E-mail: tmesales@mceducation.com
Website: www.mceducation.com

Distributed by
Singapore Math Inc.®
19535 SW 129th Avenue
Tualatin, OR 97062
Tel: (503) 557 8100
Website: www.singaporemath.com

First published 2014

Primary Mathematics (Common Core Edition) Workbook 2B
ISBN 978-981-01-9844-2

Printed in Singapore

Primary Mathematics (Common Core Edition) is adapted from Primary Mathematics Workbook 2B (3rd Edition), originally developed by the Ministry of Education, Singapore. This edition contains new content developed by Marshall Cavendish Education Pte Ltd, which is not attributable to the Ministry of Education, Singapore.

We would like to acknowledge the contributions by:

The Project Team from the Ministry of Education, Singapore that developed the original Singapore edition
Project Director: Dr Kho Tek Hong
Team Members: Hector Chee Kum Hoong, Liang Hin Hoon, Lim Eng Tann, Ng Siew Lee, Rosalind Lim Hui Cheng, Ng Hwee Wan

Primary Mathematics (Common Core Edition)
Richard Askey, Emeritus Professor of Mathematics from University of Wisconsin, Madison
Jennifer Kempe, Curriculum Advisor from Singapore Math Inc.®

CONTENTS

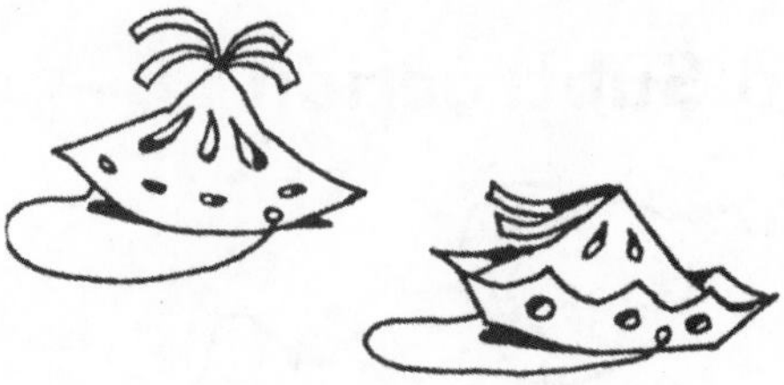

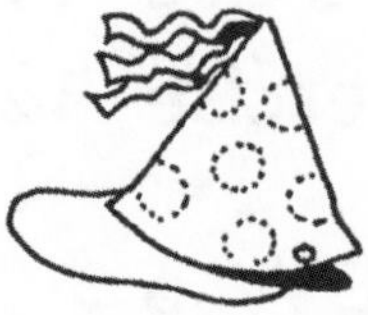

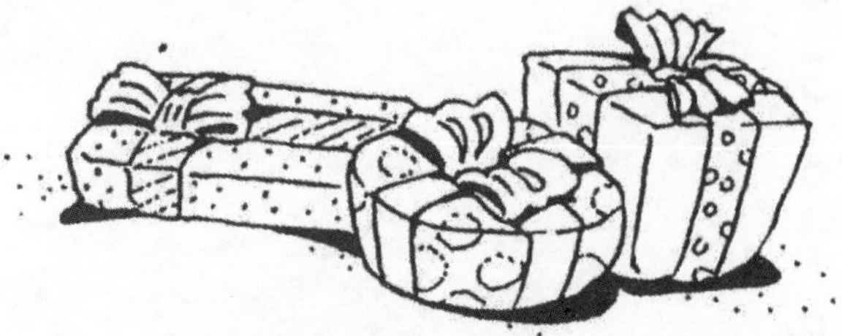

12 Geometry

EXERCISE 1

1. Write the missing numbers.

(a)

12 + ☐ = 28

(b)

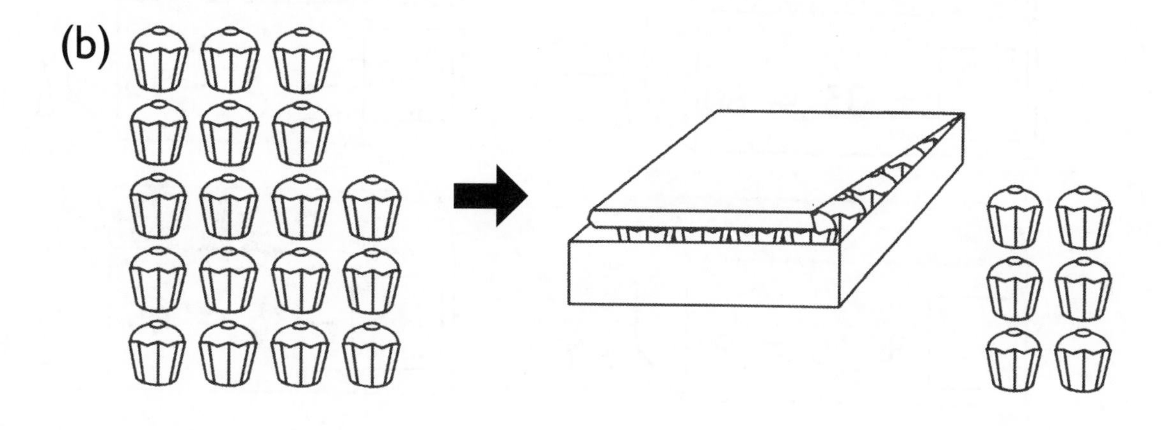

18 – ☐ = 6

(c)

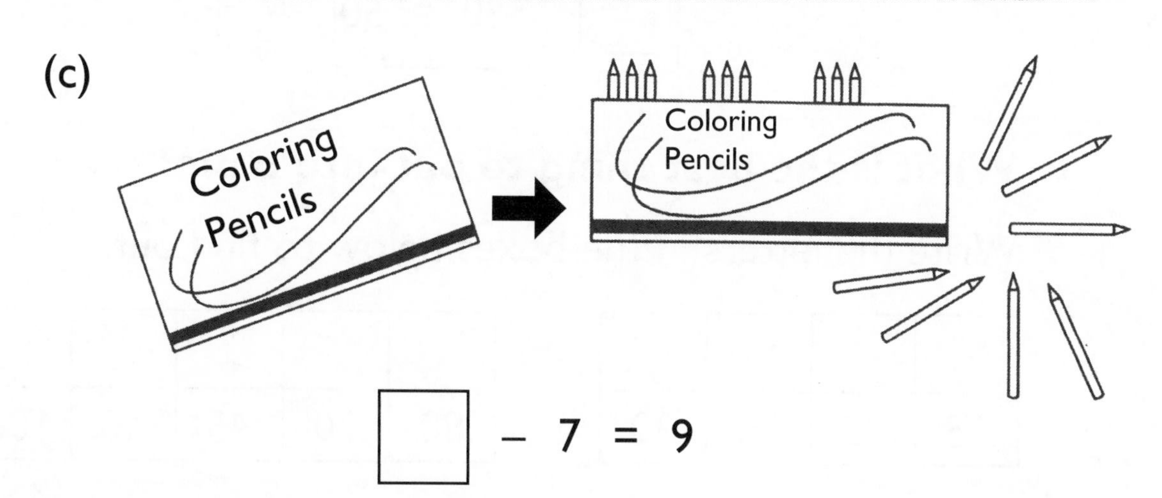

☐ – 7 = 9

2. Find the missing number in each of the following:

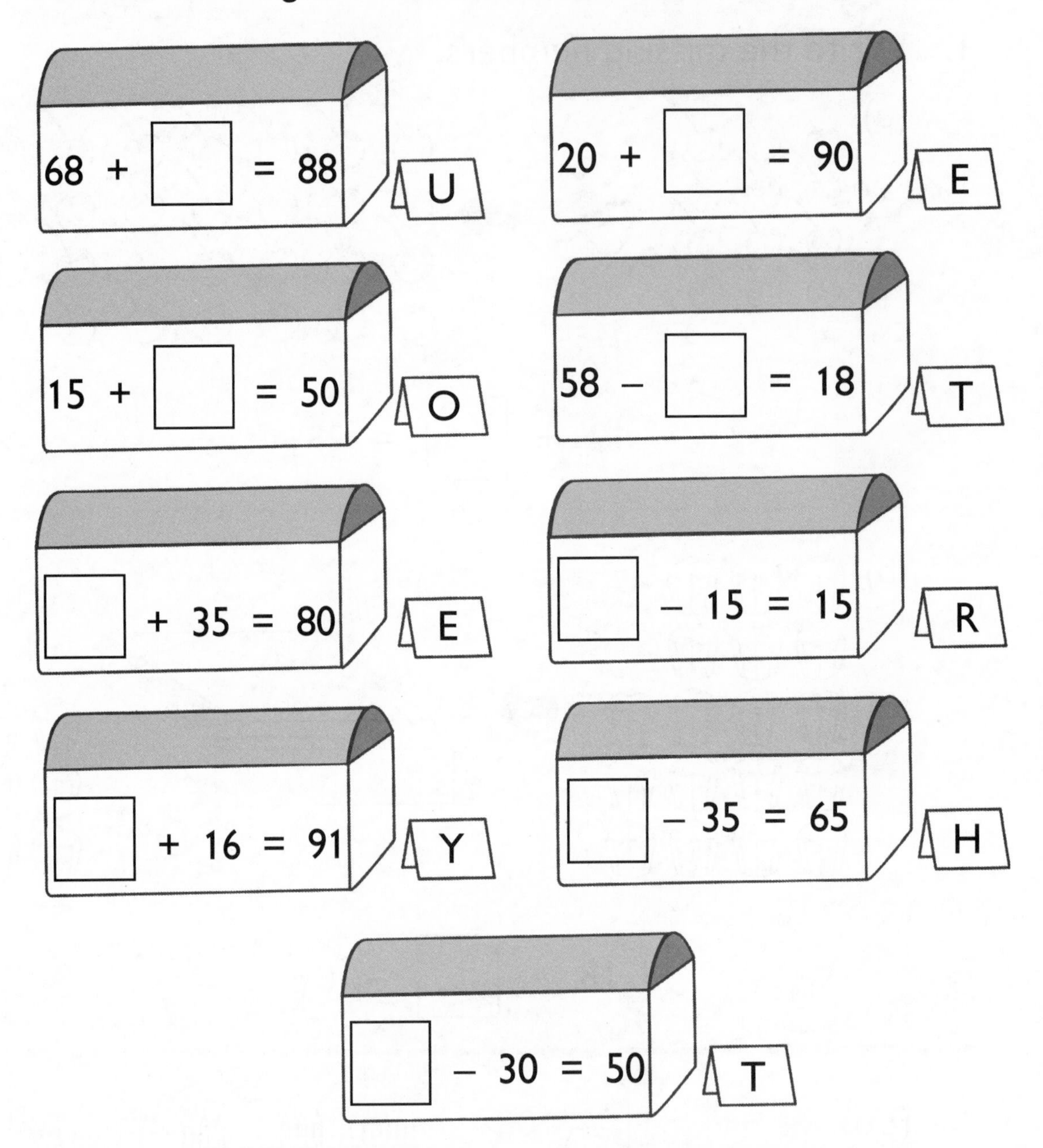

What is the best thing to put into a pie?

Write the letters in the boxes below to find out.

		U	
75	35	20	30

80	70	45	40	100

EXERCISE 2

1. Write the missing numbers.

2. Write the missing numbers.

(a) 99 + ☐ = 100	(b) 95 + ☐ = 100
(c) 96 + ☐ = 100	(d) 91 + ☐ = 100
(e) 80 + ☐ = 100	(f) 35 + ☐ = 100
(g) 84 + ☐ = 100	(h) 63 + ☐ = 100
(i) 42 + ☐ = 100	(j) 58 + ☐ = 100
(k) 6 + ☐ = 100	(l) 9 + ☐ = 100

3. Subtract.

100 – 10

100 – 40

100 – 70

4. Subtract.

(a) 100 – 98 =	(b) 100 – 93 =
(c) 100 – 85 =	(d) 100 – 27 =
(e) 100 – 79 =	(f) 100 – 56 =
(g) 100 – 22 =	(h) 100 – 34 =
(i) 100 – 9 =	(j) 100 – 7 =
(k) 100 – 1 =	(l) 100 – 4 =

EXERCISE 3

1. Write the missing numbers.

(a)

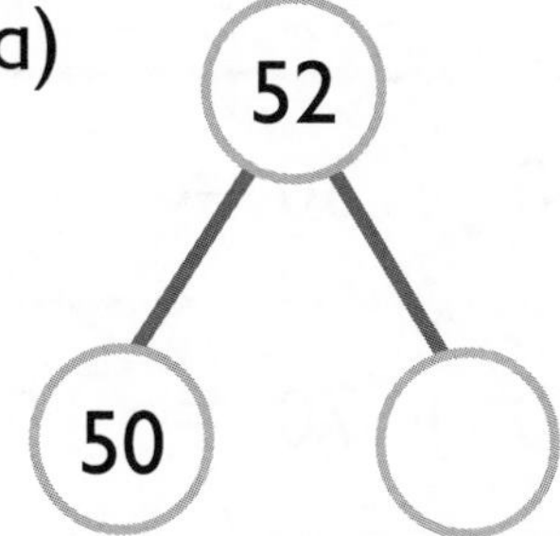

(b)

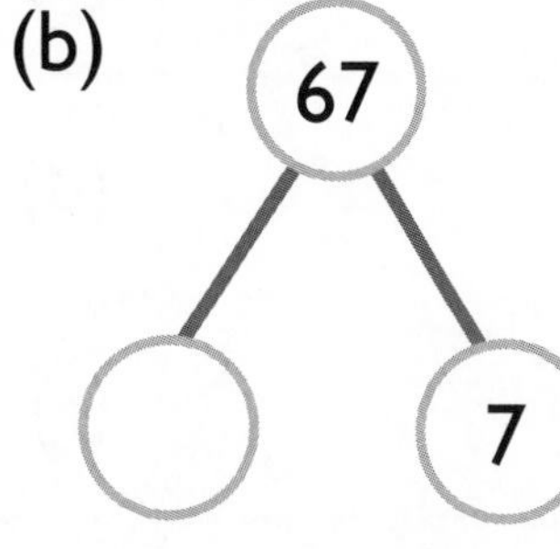

(c)

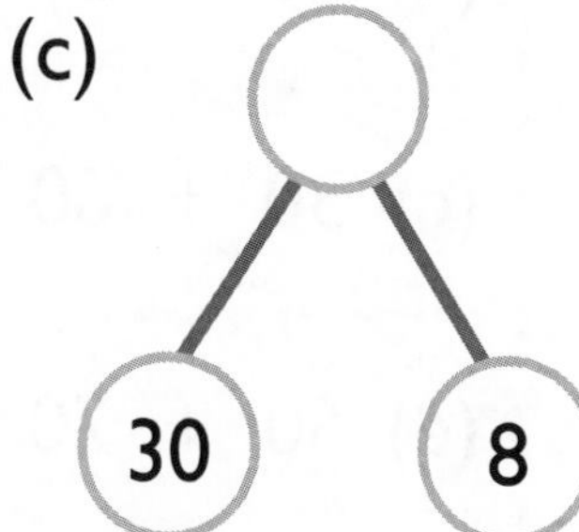

(d)

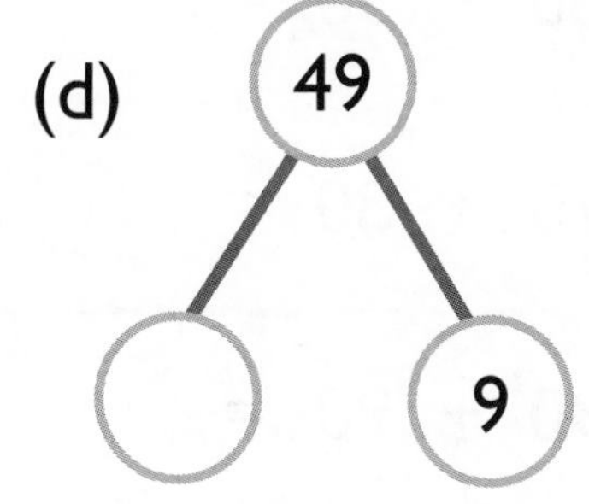

(e)

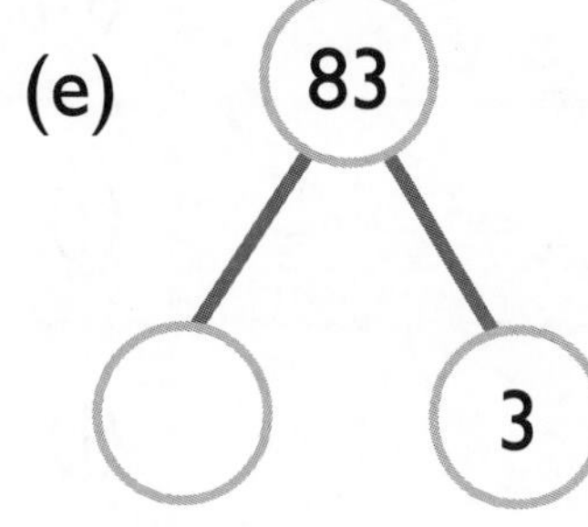

(f)

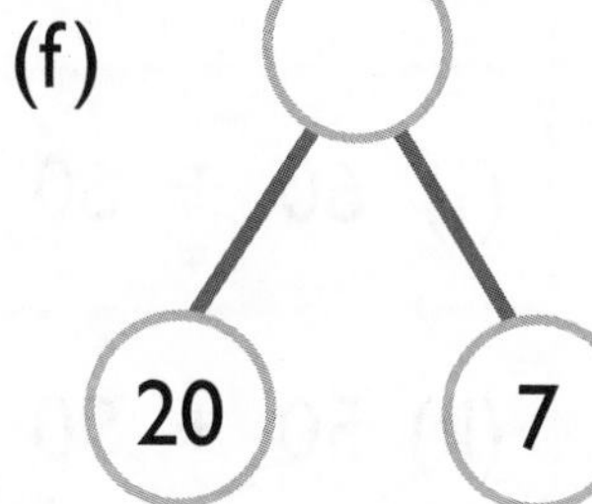

2. Add.

(a) 24 + 3 =	(b) 53 + 5 =
(c) 67 + 2 =	(d) 42 + 6 =
(e) 81 + 7 =	(f) 75 + 4 =
(g) 28 + 6 =	(h) 63 + 8 =
(i) 19 + 9 =	(j) 74 + 6 =
(k) 32 + 8 =	(l) 55 + 9 =
(m) 45 + 6 =	(n) 88 + 9 =
(o) 56 + 7 =	(p) 49 + 5 =

3. Add.

(a) 10 + 50 =	(b) 20 + 40 =
(c) 30 + 60 =	(d) 40 + 30 =
(e) 50 + 70 =	(f) 60 + 70 =
(g) 40 + 90 =	(h) 80 + 50 =
(i) 60 + 60 =	(j) 70 + 80 =
(k) 50 + 90 =	(l) 90 + 90 =

4. Add.

(a) 15 + 30 =	(b) 28 + 40 =
(c) 46 + 50 =	(d) 67 + 20 =
(e) 73 + 30 =	(f) 89 + 20 =
(g) 32 + 70 =	(h) 59 + 50 =
(i) 98 + 20 =	(j) 73 + 50 =
(k) 47 + 60 =	(l) 92 + 30 =

EXERCISE 4

1. Add.

(a) 163 + 3 =	(b) 230 + 5 =
(c) 405 + 4 =	(d) 403 + 4 =
(e) 782 + 6 =	(f) 652 + 7 =

2. Add.

(a) 135 + 6 =	(b) 187 + 9 =
(c) 354 + 8 =	(d) 408 + 7 =
(e) 563 + 9 =	(f) 656 + 8 =
(g) 738 + 5 =	(h) 289 + 9 =

3. Add.

(a) 240 + 20 =	(b) 519 + 30 =
(c) 442 + 40 =	(d) 608 + 50 =
(e) 735 + 30 =	(f) 345 + 30 =
(g) 627 + 50 =	(h) 833 + 60 =

4. Add.

(a) 250 + 60 =	(b) 410 + 90 =
(c) 638 + 90 =	(d) 545 + 70 =
(e) 386 + 80 =	(f) 875 + 80 =
(g) 775 + 70 =	(h) 690 + 90 =

5. Add.

(a) 100 + 300 =	(b) 200 + 600 =
(c) 400 + 500 =	(d) 300 + 200 =
(e) 600 + 200 =	(f) 500 + 200 =
(g) 300 + 300 =	(h) 700 + 200 =

6. Add.

(a) 350 + 100 =	(b) 506 + 200 =
(c) 375 + 300 =	(d) 409 + 500 =
(e) 264 + 300 + 100 =	(f) 325 + 200 + 200 =
(g) 415 + 300 + 200 =	(h) 435 + 400 + 100 =

EXERCISE 5

1. Write the missing numbers.

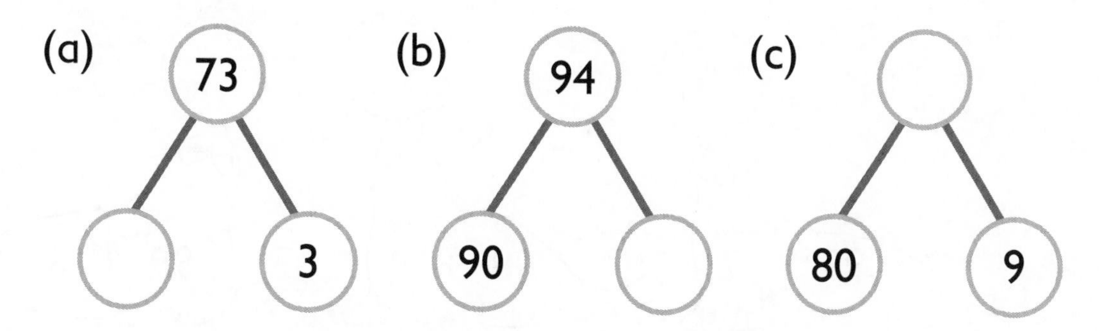

2. Write the missing numbers.

(a)

+ 30 → ( ) → + 2

40 → + 32 → ( )

(b)

+ 50 → ( ) → + 4

45 → + 54 → ( )

(c)

+ 20 → ( ) → + 3

58 → + 23 → ( )

(d)

+ 30 → ( ) → + 5

67 → + 35 → ( )

3. Add.

(a) 26 + 31 =	(b) 14 + 52 =
(c) 53 + 34 =	(d) 25 + 35 =
(e) 77 + 15 =	(f) 86 + 17 =

EXERCISE 6

1. Add.

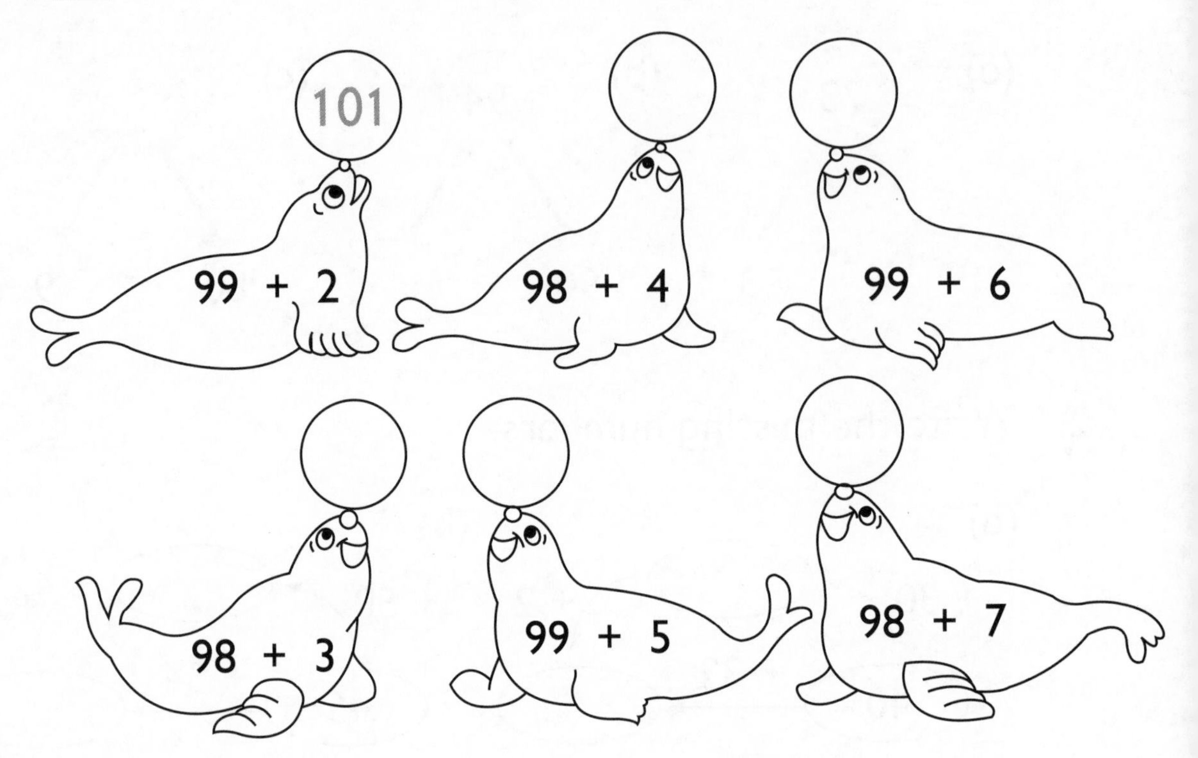

2. Add.

(a) 99 + 37 =
(b) 53 + 99 =
(c) 98 + 46 =
(d) 65 + 98 =

EXERCISE 7

1. Add.

(a) 183 + 99 =

(b) 246 + 98 =

(c) 199 + 99 =

(d) 206 + 98 =

(e) 99 + 556 =

(f) 98 + 235 =

(g) 99 + 408 =

(h) 98 + 399 =

EXERCISE 8

1. Write the missing numbers.

(a)
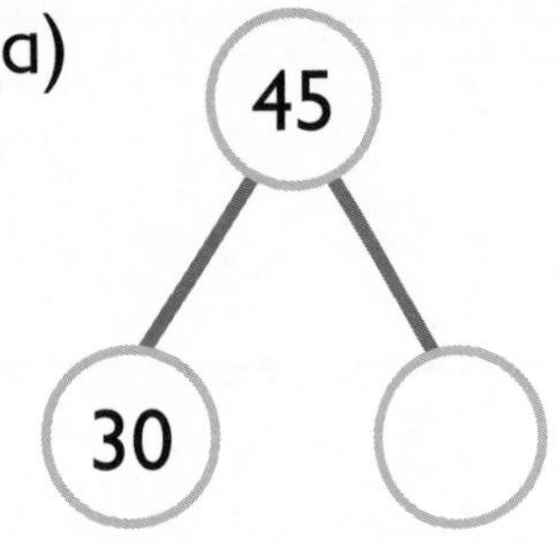

(b)
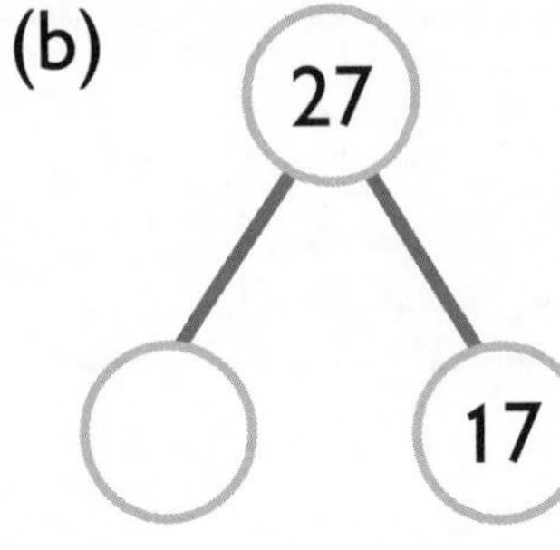

(c)
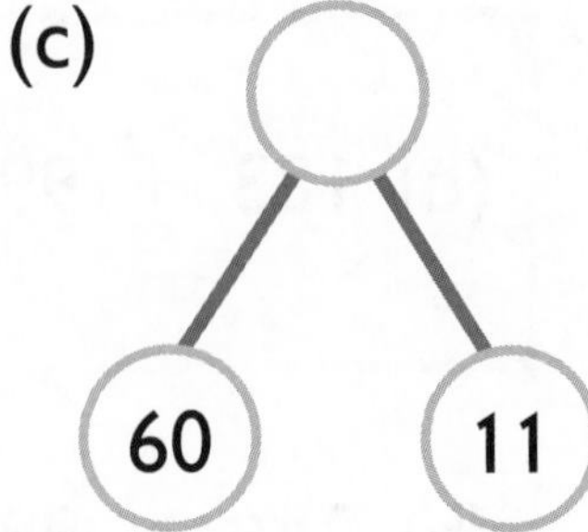

(d)
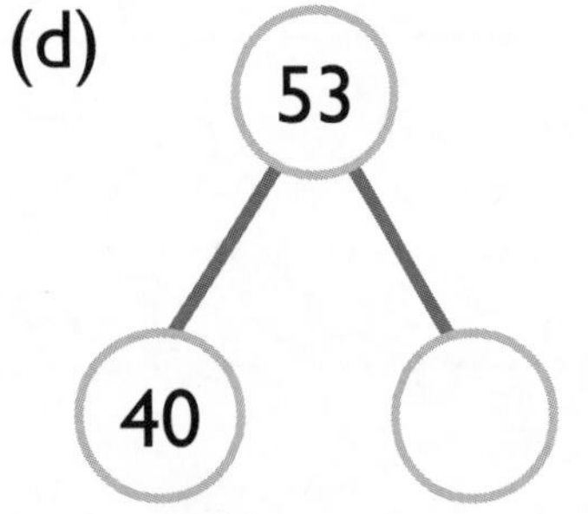

(e)
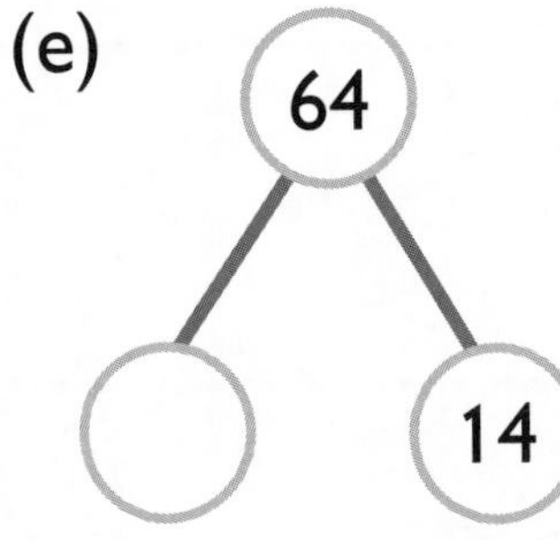

(f)
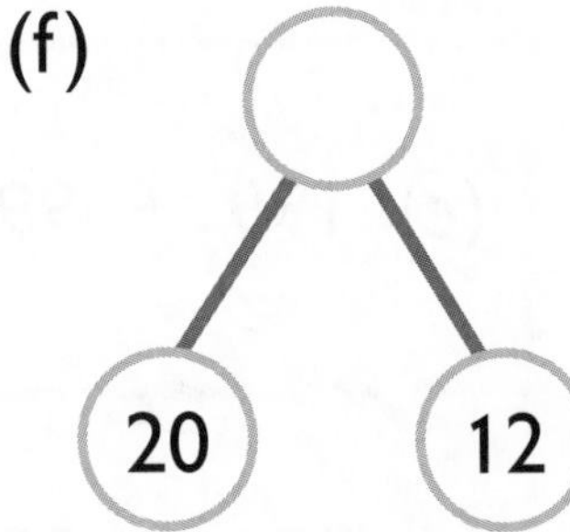

2. Subtract.

(a) 26 − 5 =	(b) 69 − 5 =
(c) 37 − 6 =	(d) 52 − 1 =
(e) 74 − 2 =	(f) 95 − 4 =
(g) 25 − 7 =	(h) 64 − 6 =
(i) 82 − 4 =	(j) 48 − 2 =
(k) 47 − 8 =	(l) 73 − 7 =
(m) 51 − 5 =	(n) 36 − 8 =
(o) 98 − 3 =	(p) 87 − 9 =

3. Subtract.

(a) 20 − 2 =	(b) 60 − 4 =
(c) 70 − 5 =	(d) 50 − 7 =
(e) 30 − 8 =	(f) 40 − 6 =
(g) 80 − 9 =	(h) 90 − 3 =

4. Subtract.

(a) 20 − 10 =	(b) 50 − 30 =
(c) 90 − 60 =	(d) 80 − 40 =
(e) 60 − 50 =	(f) 30 − 20 =
(g) 40 − 40 =	(h) 70 − 60 =

5. Subtract.

(a) 51 − 30 =	(b) 73 − 40 =
(c) 87 − 60 =	(d) 68 − 50 =
(e) 44 − 30 =	(f) 35 − 10 =
(g) 79 − 20 =	(h) 92 − 80 =

EXERCISE 9

1. Subtract.

(a) 877 − 5 =	(b) 938 − 4 =
(c) 415 − 3 =	(d) 269 − 7 =
(e) 104 − 1 =	(f) 655 − 2 =

2. Subtract.

(a) 450 − 8 =	(b) 683 − 5 =
(c) 891 − 3 =	(d) 565 − 9 =
(e) 236 − 8 =	(f) 950 − 6 =
(g) 722 − 4 =	(h) 144 − 7 =

3. Subtract.

(a) 583 − 80 =	(b) 767 − 10 =
(c) 161 − 40 =	(d) 357 − 30 =
(e) 280 − 50 =	(f) 876 − 70 =
(g) 692 − 60 =	(h) 448 − 20 =

4. Subtract.

(a) 539 – 70 =	(b) 748 – 90 =
(c) 266 – 80 =	(d) 353 – 70 =
(e) 407 – 30 =	(f) 625 – 80 =
(g) 238 – 40 =	(h) 831 – 60 =

5. Subtract.

(a) 400 – 300 =	(b) 700 – 500 =
(c) 900 – 200 =	(d) 300 – 100 =
(e) 800 – 400 =	(f) 600 – 300 =
(g) 200 – 100 =	(h) 500 – 200 =

6. Subtract.

(a) 833 – 400 =	(b) 389 – 300 =
(c) 253 – 100 =	(d) 594 – 200 =
(e) 735 – 500 =	(f) 627 – 400 =
(g) 486 – 200 =	(h) 768 – 600 =

EXERCISE 10

1. Write the missing numbers.

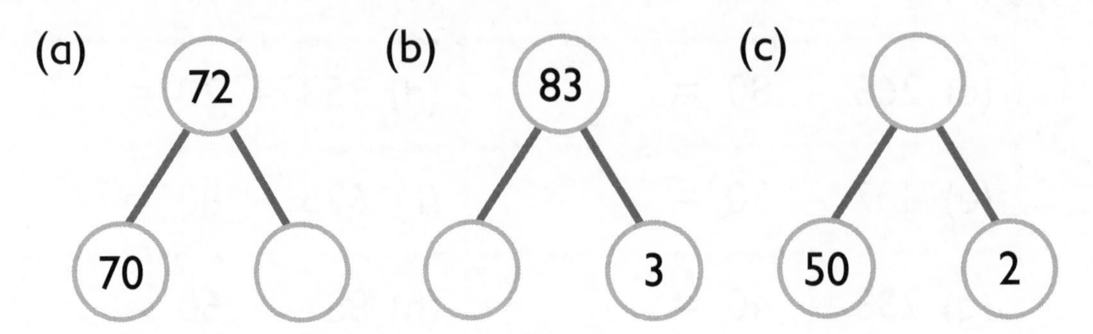

2. Write the missing numbers.

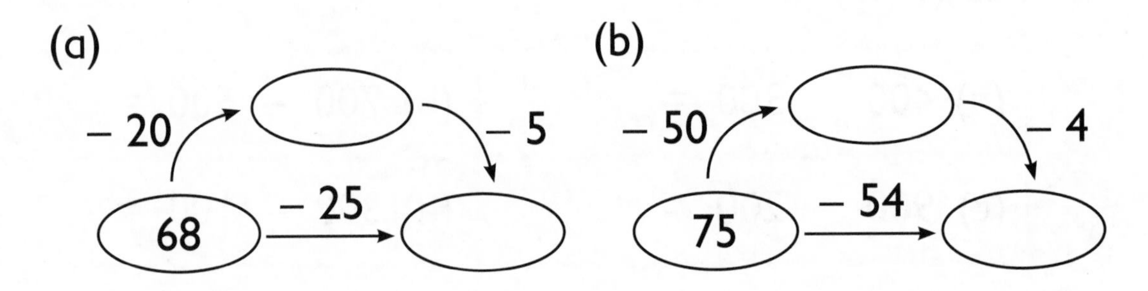

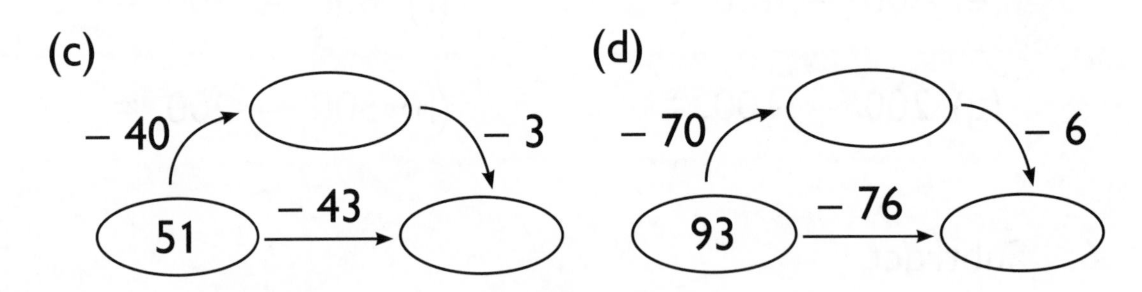

3. Subtract.

(a) 74 – 32 =	(b) 69 – 57 =
(c) 87 – 64 =	(d) 55 – 46 =
(e) 46 – 28 =	(f) 35 – 17 =

4. Write the missing numbers.

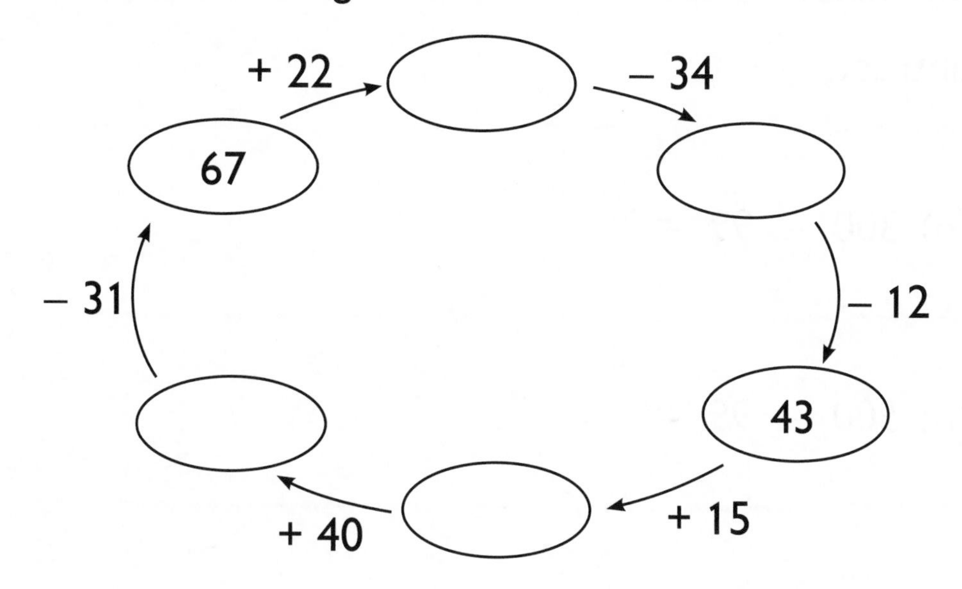

5. Add or subtract.

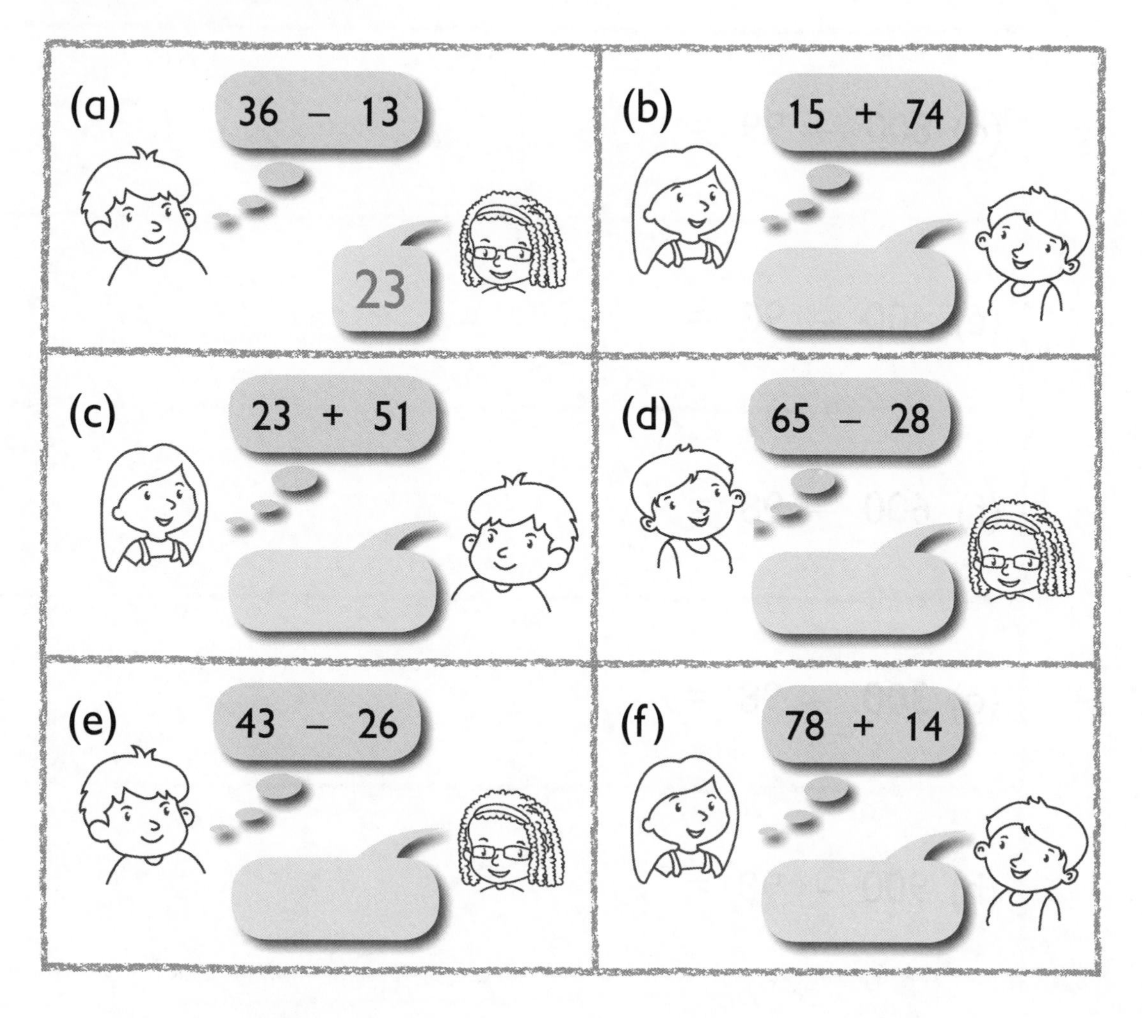

EXERCISE 11

1. Subtract.

(a) 300 − 99 =
(b) 500 − 99 =
(c) 700 − 99 =
(d) 800 − 99 =
(e) 400 − 98 =
(f) 600 − 98 =
(g) 300 − 98 =
(h) 900 − 98 =

EXERCISE 12

1. Subtract.

(a) 180 − 99 =

(b) 302 − 99 =

(c) 556 − 99 =

(d) 848 − 99 =

(e) 205 − 98 =

(f) 467 − 98 =

(g) 780 − 98 =

(h) 632 − 98 =

REVIEW 6

1. Write the missing numbers.

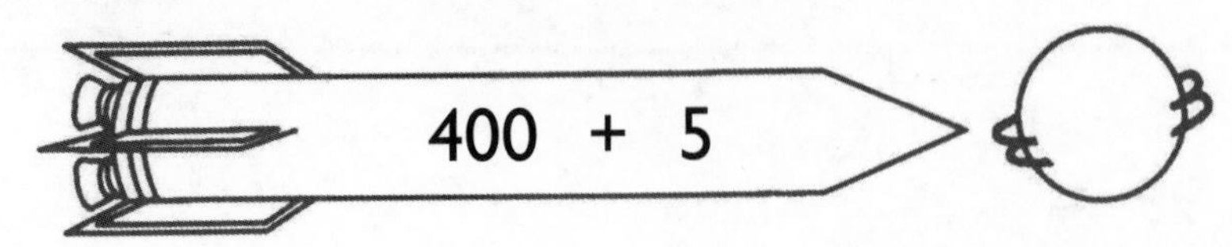

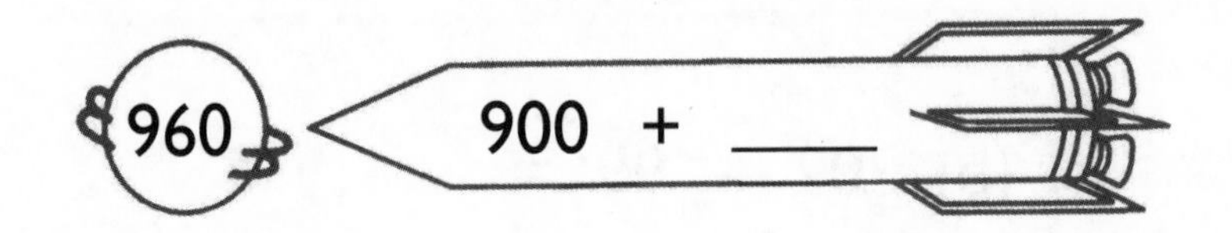

2. Write the missing numbers.

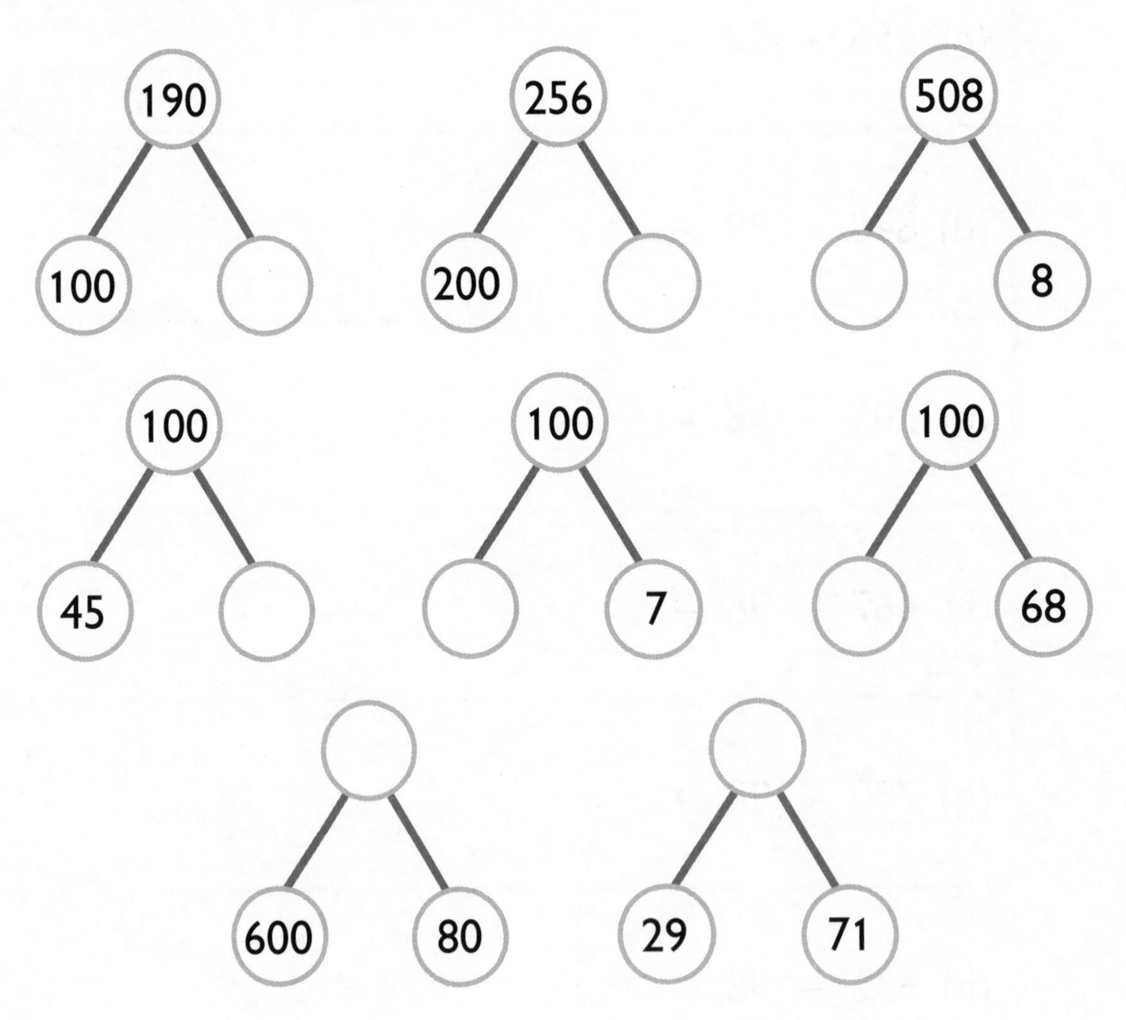

3. Add or Subtract.

(a) $34 + 14 =$

(b) $99 + 26 =$

(c) $135 + 40 =$

(d) $350 + 200 =$

(e) $65 - 45 =$

(f) $284 - 30 =$

(g) $345 - 23 =$

(h) $300 - 98 =$

EXERCISE 1

1. Count by 4s.

2. Fill in the blanks by counting on or back.

(a) 4, 8, 12, ____, ____.

(b) 24, 28, ____, ____, 40.

(c) 36, 32, ____, ____, 20.

(d) 16, ____, ____, 4.

3. Complete the multiplication sentences.

(a)	Multiply 4 by 1.	$4 \times 1 =$
(b)	Multiply 4 by 2.	$4 \times 2 =$
(c)	Multiply 4 by 3.	$4 \times 3 =$
(d)	Multiply 4 by 4.	$4 \times 4 =$
(e)	Multiply 4 by 5.	$4 \times 5 =$

(f) Multiply 4 by 6.

$4 \times 6 =$

(g) Multiply 4 by 7.

$4 \times 7 =$

(h) Multiply 4 by 8.

$4 \times 8 =$

(i) Multiply 4 by 9.

$4 \times 9 =$

(j) Multiply 4 by 10.

$4 \times 10 =$

EXERCISE 2

1. Complete the multiplication equations.

(a)

$2 \times 4 =$

$4 \times 2 =$

(b)

$3 \times 4 =$

$4 \times 3 =$

(c)

$7 \times 4 =$

$4 \times 7 =$

(d)

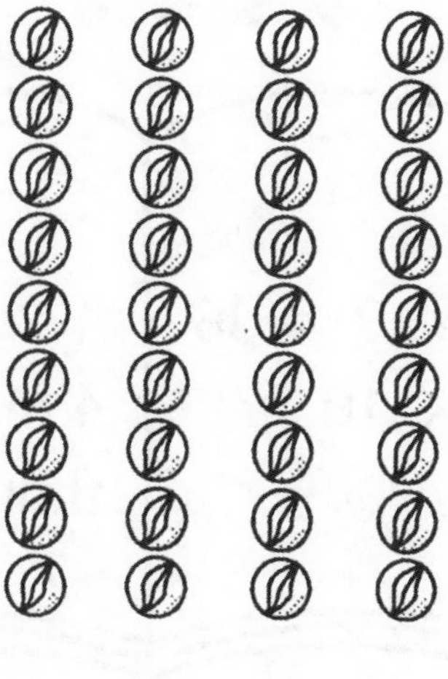

$9 \times 4 =$

$4 \times 9 =$

2. Complete the multiplication equations.

(a)

8

$4 \times 2 = 8$
$4 \times 3 =$

4×3 is 4 more than 8.

(b)

20

$4 \times 5 = 20$
$4 \times 6 =$

4×6 is 4 more than 20.

(c)

16

$4 \times 4 = 16$
$4 \times 5 =$

4×5 is 4 more than 16.

(d)

36

$4 \times 9 = 36$
$4 \times 10 =$

4×10 is 4 more than 36.

3. Complete the multiplication equations.

$4 \times 3 = 12$
$4 \times 4 =$

4×4 is 4 more than 12.

$4 \times 7 = 28$
$4 \times 8 =$

4×8 is 4 more than 28.

$4 \times 6 = 24$
$4 \times 7 =$

4×7 is 4 more than 24.

$4 \times 8 = 32$
$4 \times 9 =$

4×9 is 4 more than 32.

$4 \times 6 = 24$
$4 \times 5 =$

4×5 is 4 less than 24.

$4 \times 8 = 32$
$4 \times 7 =$

4×7 is 4 less than 32.

4. Match the spaceships and the robots.

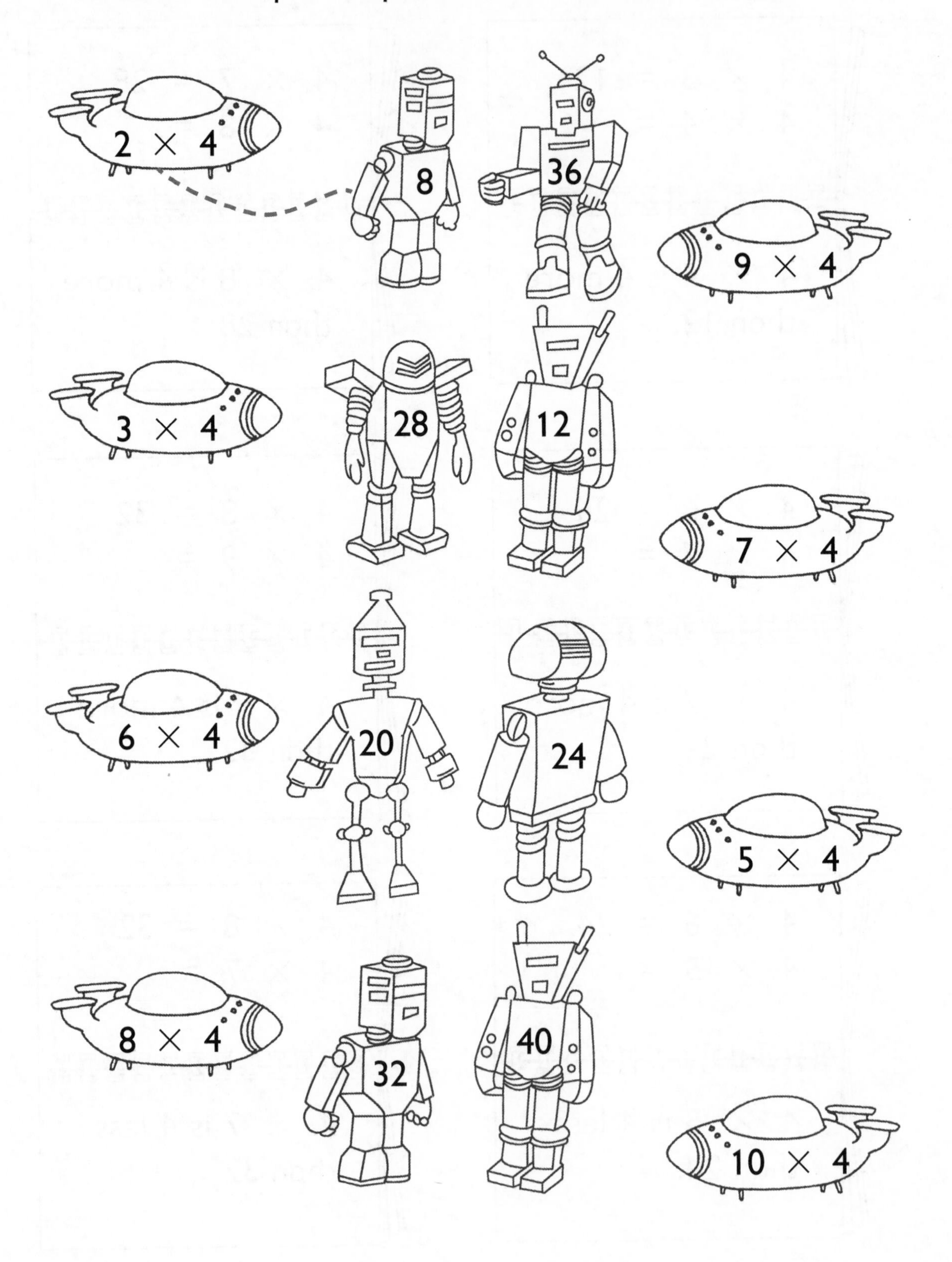

5. Multiply.

4×2 = 8

4×7

4×5

4×8

4×4

6×4

1×4

10×4

4×3

4×9

EXERCISE 3

1. Mr. Smith planted 4 rows of trees.
   There were 5 trees in each row.
   How many trees were there altogether?

   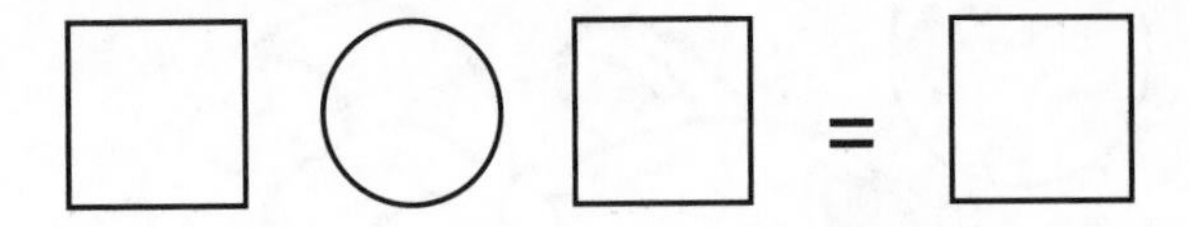

   There were ________ trees altogether.

---

2. The length of each side of the square is 6 cm.
   What is the total length of the
   4 sides of the square?

   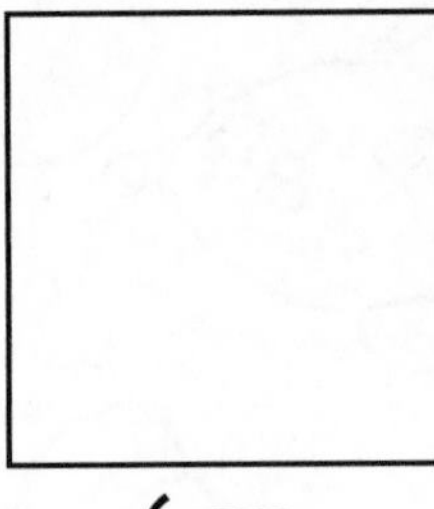

---

3. 4 boys went fishing.
   Each boy caught 3 fish.
   How many fish did they catch altogether?

4. Denisha bought 6 T-shirts.
Each T-shirt cost $4.
How much did Denisha pay altogether?

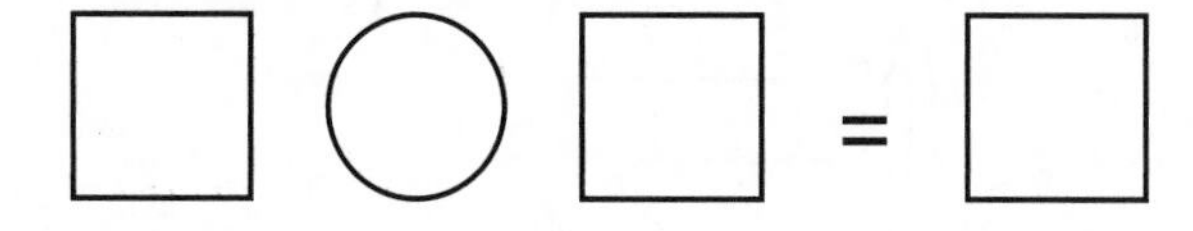

Denisha paid $________ altogether.

---

5. Ms. Young bought 9 pieces of cloth.
Each piece of cloth was 4 m long.
How many meters of cloth did Ms. Young buy?

---

6. Mr. Coles bought 10 bottles of milk.
Each bottle cost $4.
How much did Mr. Coles pay?

EXERCISE 4

1. Write the missing numbers.

$1 \times 4 = 4$

$4 \div 4 =$

$2 \times 4 = 8$

$8 \div 4 =$

$3 \times 4 = 12$

$12 \div 4 =$

$\times 4 = 16$

$16 \div 4 =$

$\times 4 = 20$

$20 \div 4 =$

$\times 4 = 24$

$24 \div 4 =$

$\times 4 = 40$

$40 \div 4 =$

$\times 4 = 28$

$28 \div 4 =$

$\times 4 = 36$

$36 \div 4 =$

$\times 4 = 32$

$32 \div 4 =$

2. Match the frogs to the correct tadpoles.

EXERCISE 5

1. 36 children lined up in 4 equal rows.
   How many children were there in each row?

2. Larry bought 4 bunches of grapes.
   He paid $24.
   What was the cost of 1 bunch of grapes?

3. 4 pieces of ribbon are of the same length.
   Their total length is 28 m.
   How long is each piece of ribbon?

4. Peter has 14 coins.
   He wants to put as many coins as possible into 4 equal groups.
   (a) How many coins are there in each group?

   (b) Are there any coins left over?

---

5. Mary has 26 beads and some pieces of string.
   She puts 4 beads on each string.
   How many beads are left over?

---

6. Natalie has a ribbon that is 37 in. long.
   She cuts it into pieces 4 in. long each.
   How many inches of ribbon are left over?

EXERCISE 6

1. Count by 5s

2. Fill in the blanks by counting by 5s.

   (a) 5, 10, 15, ________, ________.

   (b) 25, 30, ________, ________, 45.

3. Complete the multiplication equations.

5 × 3 is 5 more than 10.

$5 \times 1 = 5$

$5 \times 2 = 10$

$5 \times 3 =$

$5 \times 4 =$

$5 \times 5 =$

$5 \times 6 =$

$5 \times 7 =$

$5 \times 8 =$

$5 \times 9 =$

$5 \times 10 =$

EXERCISE 7

1. Complete the multiplication equations.

(a)

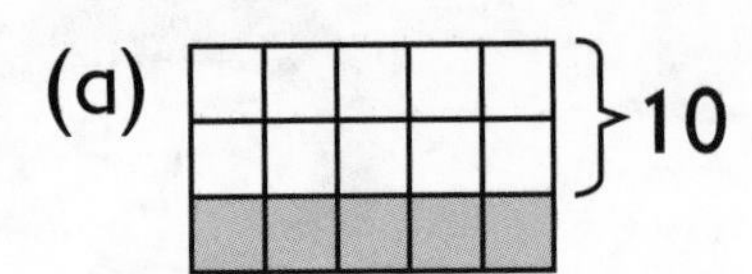

$5 \times 2 = 10$

$5 \times 3 =$ ⟵ 5 more than 10

(b)

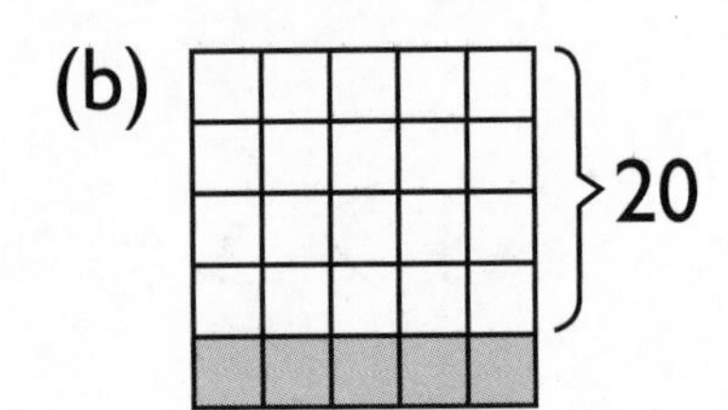

$5 \times 4 = 20$

$5 \times 5 =$ ⟵ 5 more than 20

(c)

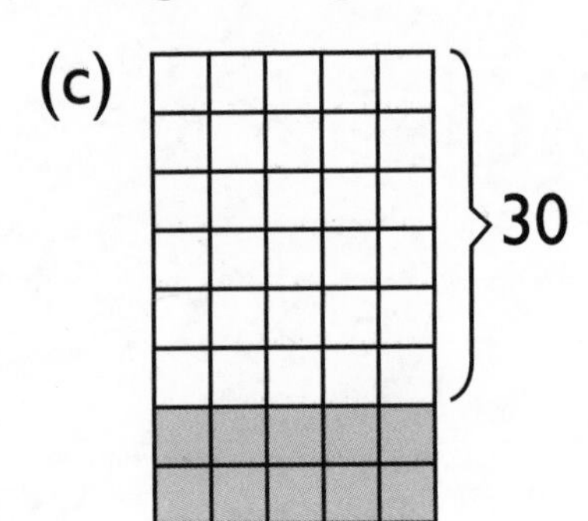

$5 \times 6 = 30$

$5 \times 8 =$ ⟵ 10 more than 30

(d)

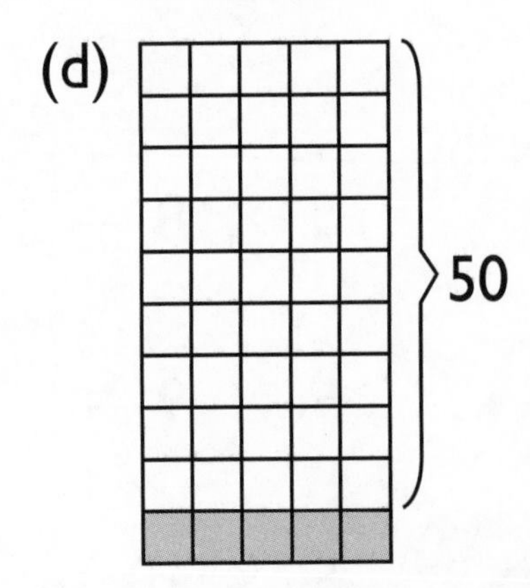

$5 \times 10 = 50$

$5 \times 9 =$ ⟵ 5 less than 50

2. Match the boats and flags.

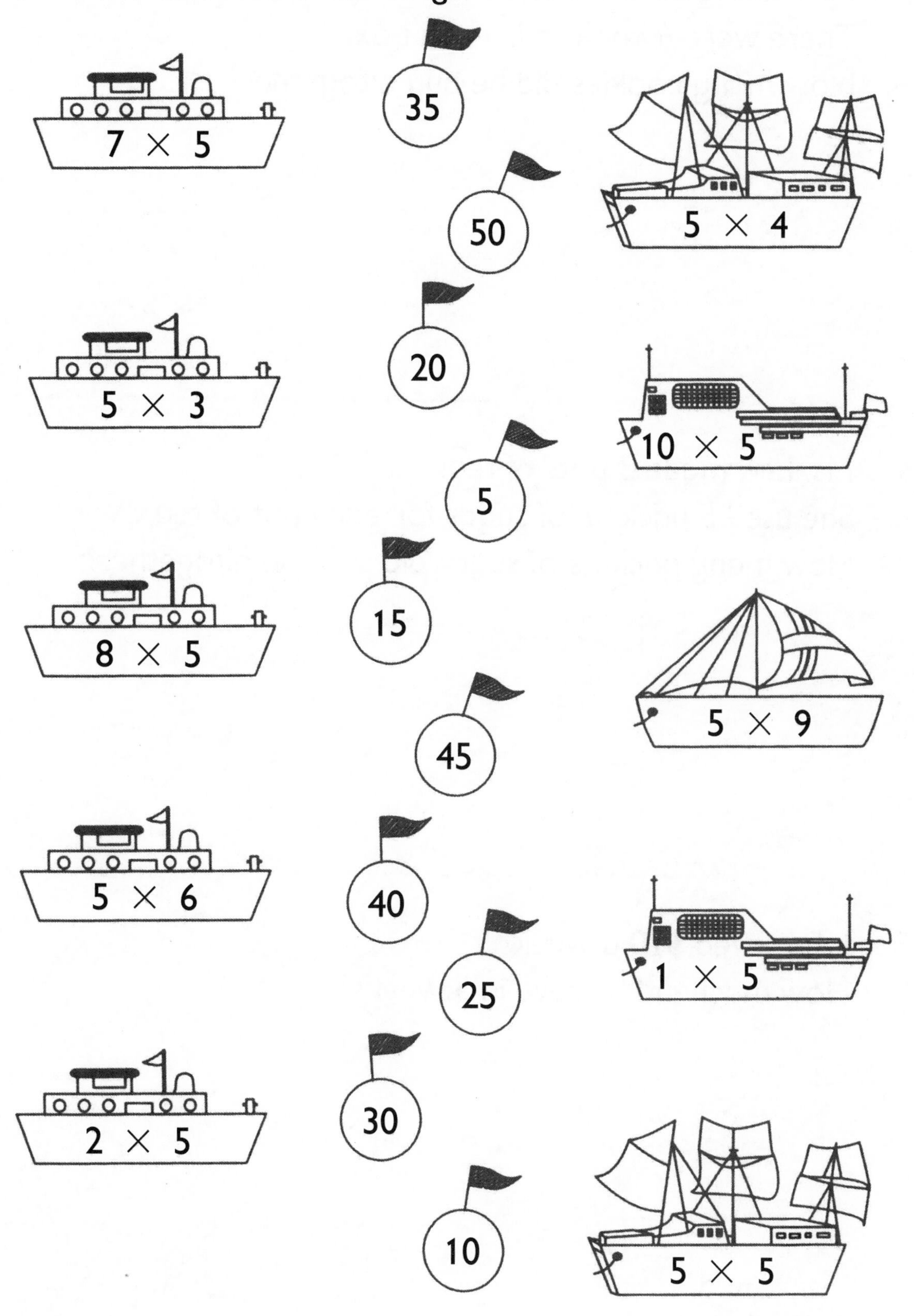

3. Mr. Rodriguez bought 5 boxes of cookies.
There were 6 cookies in each box.
How many cookies did he buy altogether?

---

4. Ms. Levi made 3 pots of tea.
She used 5 packets of sugar for each pot of tea.
How many packets of sugar did she use altogether?

---

5. John saved $10 a week.
How much did he save in 5 weeks?

6. Jason had 5 trays of chocolate cupcakes.
   There were 7 cupcakes on each tray.
   How many cupcakes were there altogether?

---

7. Jack and Jill each had 5 bean seeds to plant.
   How many seeds did they have in all?

EXERCISE 8

1. Write the missing numbers.

$1 \times 5 = 5$

$5 \div 5 =$

$2 \times 5 = 10$

$10 \div 5 =$

$3 \times 5 = 15$

$15 \div 5 =$

$\times 5 = 35$

$35 \div 5 =$

$\times 5 = 25$

$25 \div 5 =$

$\times 5 = 45$

$45 \div 5 =$

$\times 5 = 20$

$20 \div 5 =$

$\times 5 = 30$

$30 \div 5 =$

$\times 5 = 40$

$40 \div 5 =$

$\times 5 = 50$

$50 \div 5 =$

2. Match the fish and hooks.

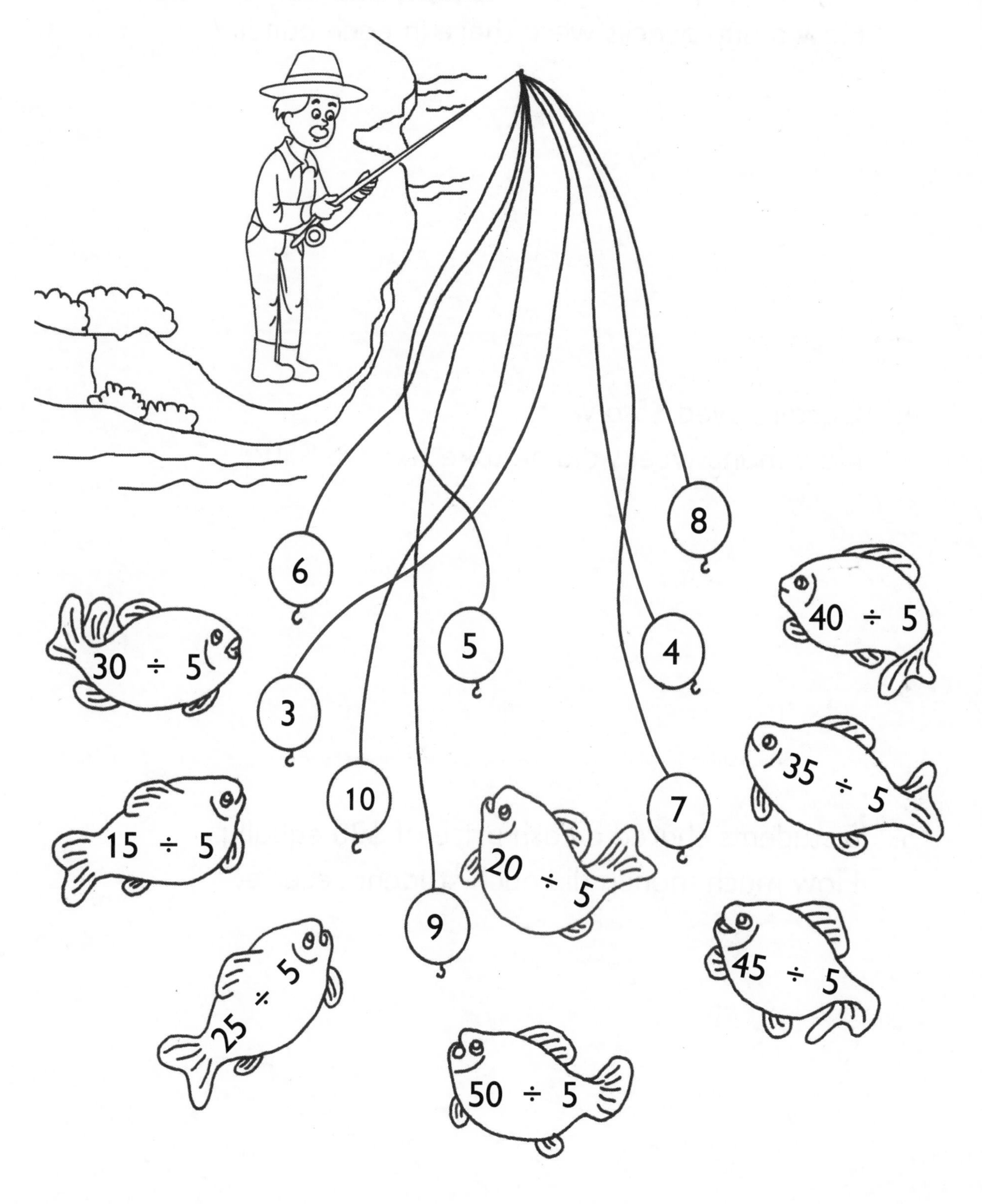

3. Lily tied 40 pencils into 5 equal bundles.
How many pencils were there in each bundle?

4. Carter saved $5 a week.
How many weeks did he take to save $50?

5. 5 students shared a cash prize of $20 equally.
How much money did each student receive?

6. Tim has 16 counters.
   He wants to put as many counters as possible into 5 equal groups.

   (a) How many counters are there in each group?

   (b) Are there any counters left over?

---

7. Susan has 26 eggs.
   She wants to pack 5 eggs onto each tray.

   (a) How many trays will she need?

   (b) How many eggs will she have left over?

---

8. Bill has a rope that is 37 m long.
   He wants to cut it into pieces that are 7 m long each.

   (a) How many pieces of rope he get?

   (b) How many meters of rope will be left over?

EXERCISE 9

1. Count by 10s.

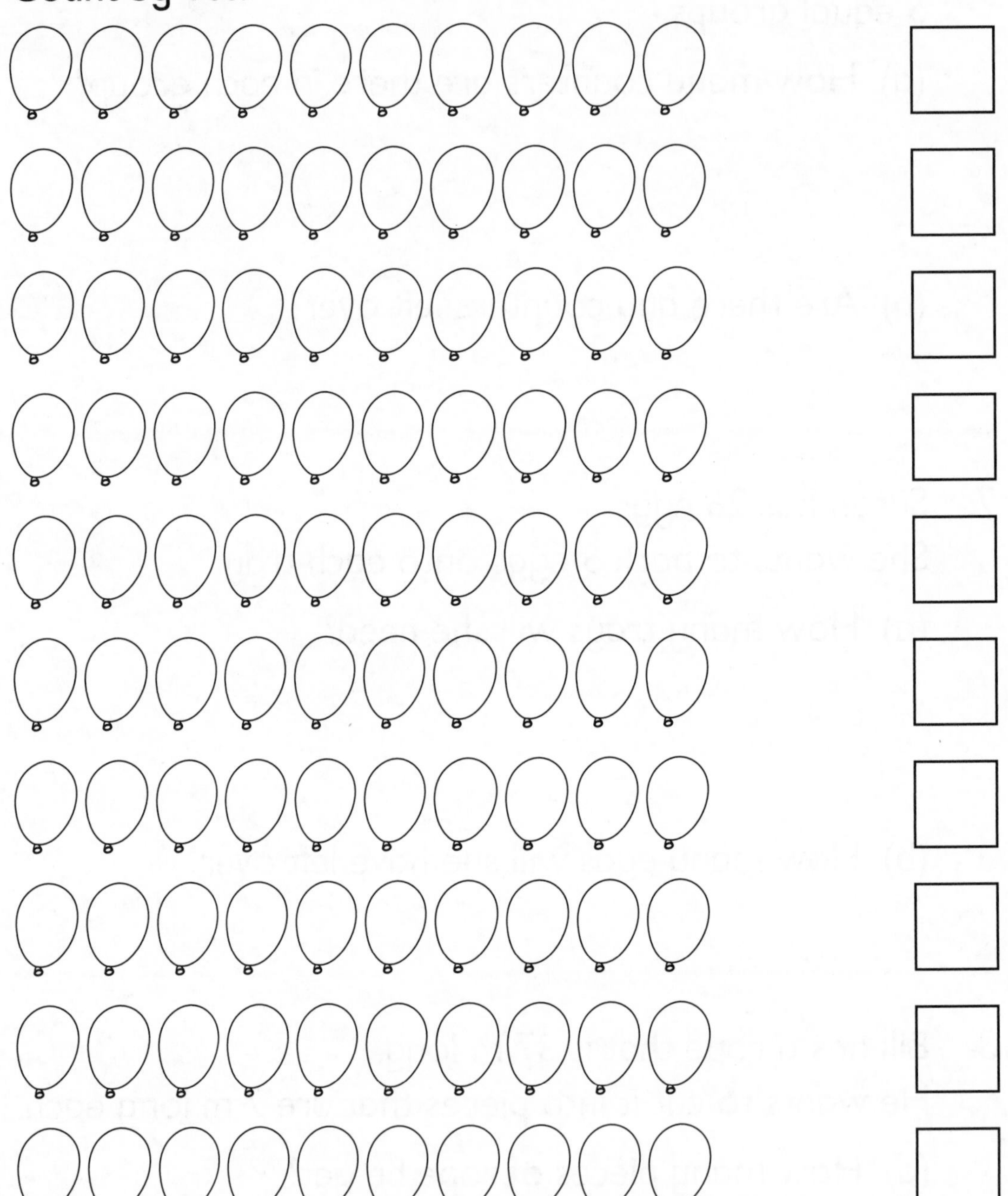

2. Fill in the blanks by counting by 10s.

(a) 10, 20, 30, ________, ________.

(b) 60, ________, ________, 90, 100.

3. Complete the multiplication equations.

10×3 is 10 more than 20.

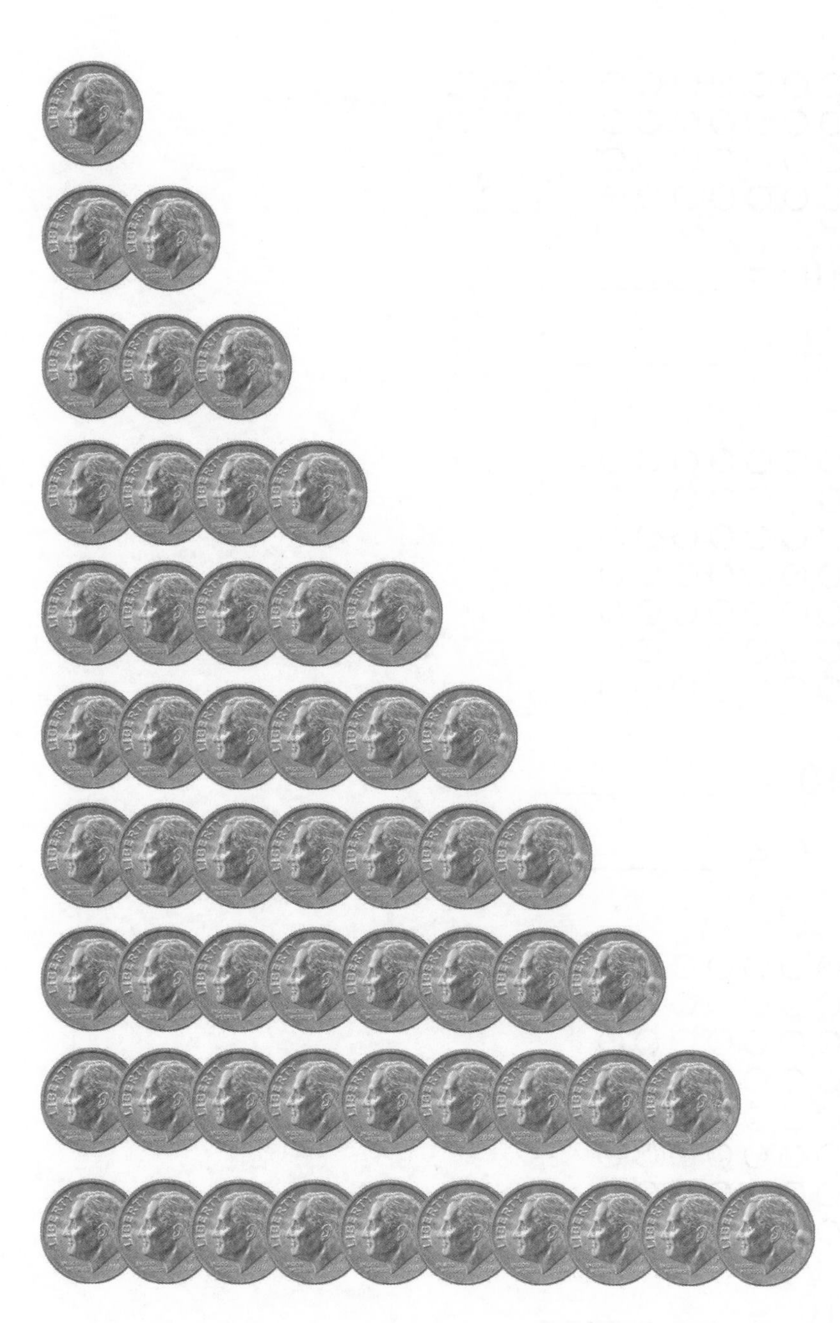

$10 \times 1 = 10$

$10 \times 2 = 20$

$10 \times 3 =$

$10 \times 4 =$

$10 \times 5 =$

$10 \times 6 =$

$10 \times 7 =$

$10 \times 8 =$

$10 \times 9 =$

$10 \times 10 =$

4. Complete the multiplication equations.

(a) ○○○○○○○○○○
○○○○○○○○○○

$2 \times 10 =$ ________

$10 \times 2 =$ ________

(b) ○○○○○○○○○○
○○○○○○○○○○
○○○○○○○○○○
○○○○○○○○○○

$4 \times 10 =$ ________

$10 \times 4 =$ ________

(c) ○○○○○○○○○○
○○○○○○○○○○
○○○○○○○○○○
○○○○○○○○○○
○○○○○○○○○○
○○○○○○○○○○
○○○○○○○○○○

$7 \times 10 =$ ________

$10 \times 7 =$ ________

(d) ○○○○○○○○○○
○○○○○○○○○○
○○○○○○○○○○
○○○○○○○○○○
○○○○○○○○○○
○○○○○○○○○○
○○○○○○○○○○
○○○○○○○○○○

$8 \times 10 =$ ________

$10 \times 8 =$ ________

5. There are 5 trees in each row.
Each row has the same number of trees.
How many trees are there in 10 rows?

---

6. A raffle ticket cost $10.
Mr. Smith sold 10 tickets.
How much money did he receive?

---

7. Ms. Wells bought 10 m of cloth to make dresses.
1 m of cloth cost $7.
How much did Ms. Wells pay?

EXERCISE 10

1. Write the missing numbers.

$3 \times 10 = 30$ — $30 \div 10 =$

$\times 10 = 50$ — $50 \div 10 =$

$\times 10 = 60$ — $60 \div 10 =$

$\times 10 = 70$ — $70 \div 10 =$

$\times 10 = 10$ — $10 \div 10 =$

$10 \times \quad = 30$ — $30 \div 10 =$

$10 \times \quad = 80$ — $80 \div 10 =$

$10 \times \quad = 40$ — $40 \div 10 =$

$10 \times \quad = 20$ — $20 \div 10 =$

$10 \times \quad = 90$ — $90 \div 10 =$

2. Match each mother bird with its egg.

3. The total cost of 10 bags of flour is $60.
   What is the cost of 1 bag of flour?

4. Mr. Goldman paid $40 for 10 potted plants.
   What was the cost of 1 potted plant?

5. There are 80 marbles altogether in 10 boxes.
   Each box has an equal number of marbles.
   How many marbles are there in each box?

6. Rani has 94 beads and 9 pieces of string.
   She puts 10 beads on each string.
   How many beads are left over?

---

7. Brenda has 65 cherries.
   She places 10 cherries on each of her 6 cakes.
   How many cherries are left over?

---

8. Mrs. Harries buys 34 pencils.
   She gives away 3 pencils to each of her 10 pupils.
   How many pencils does she have left over?

REVIEW 7

1. Fill in the blanks.

   (a) 16, 20, 24, ________, ________.

   (b) 40, 50, 60, ________, ________.

   (c) 30, 35, ________, ________, 50.

2. Complete the multiplication equations.

   (a)

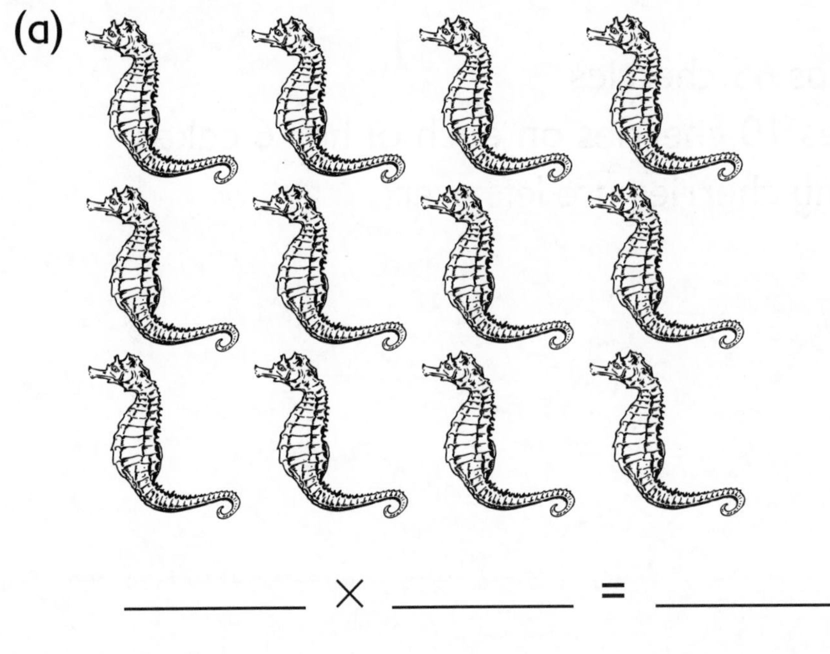

________ × ________ = ________

________ × ________ = ________

   (b)

________ × ________ = ________

________ × ________ = ________

(c) 

_____ × _____ = _____

_____ × _____ = _____

(d)

_____ × _____ = _____

_____ × _____ = _____

3. Multiply or divide.

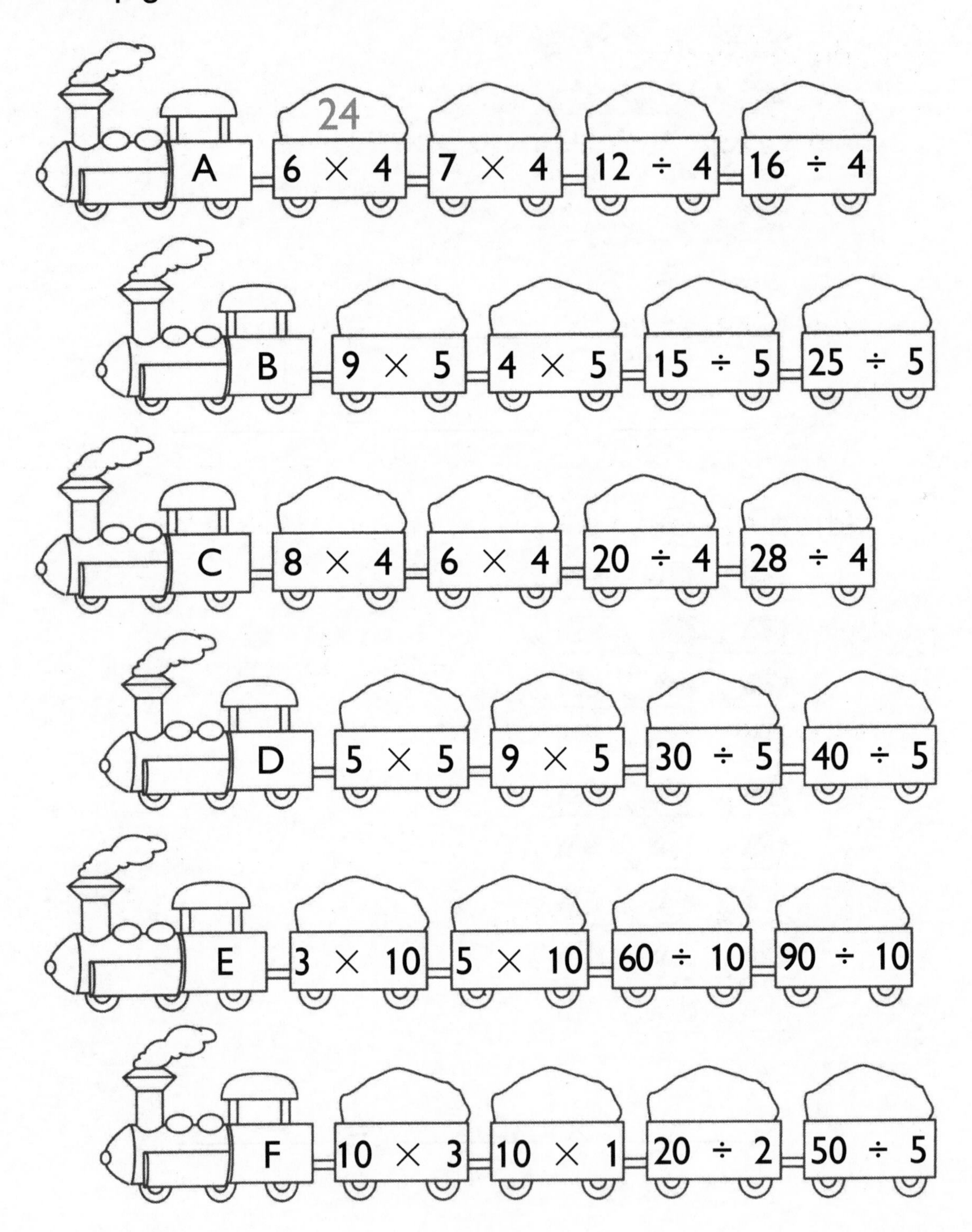

4. Jo arranges 4 rows of tables.
   There are 9 tables in each row.
   How many tables are there altogether?

---

5. Sam bought 3 boxes of pencils.
   There were 10 pencils in each box.
   How many pencils were there altogether?

---

6. A boat can carry 5 people.
   How many boats are needed to carry 43 people?

7. 1 bag of peaches costs $5.
What is the cost of 9 bags of peaches?

---

8. Moby paid $60 for 10 similar T-shirts.
How much did each T-shirt cost?

---

9. Each van can carry 10 pupils.
There are 50 pupils.
How many vans are needed?

10. Jason has 35 marbles.
He wants to place 4 marbles in each box.
(a) How many boxes will he need?

(b) How many marbles will be left over?

---

11. Jack has 17 markers.
He wants to put as many markers as possible into 5 equal groups.
(a) How many markers are there in each group?

(b) How many markers are left over?

---

12. Paula has 53 candles.
She places 10 candles equally on each of her candle holders.
How many candles are left over?

EXERCISE 1

1. Match the bags with the price tags.

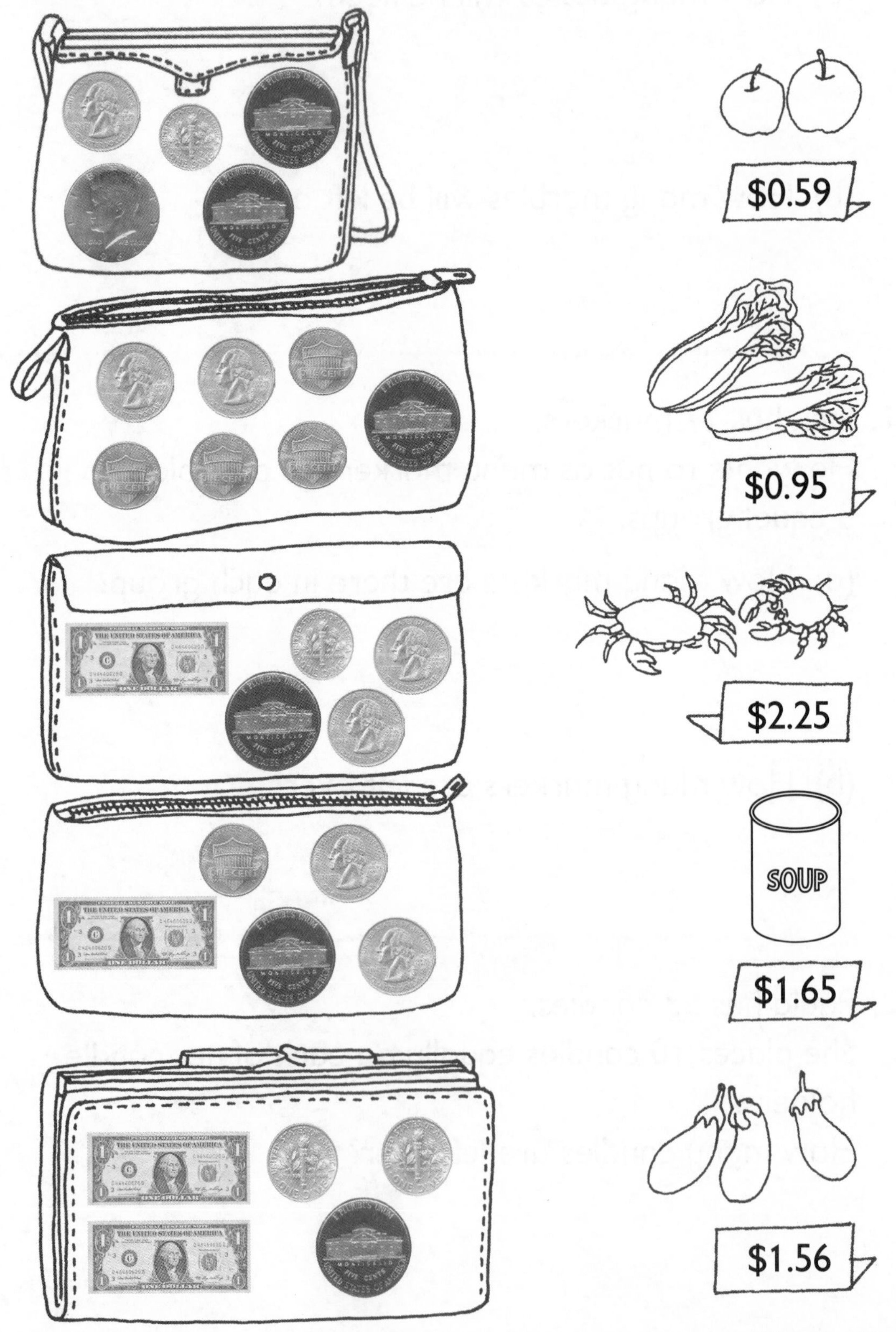

2. How much money is there in each of the following?

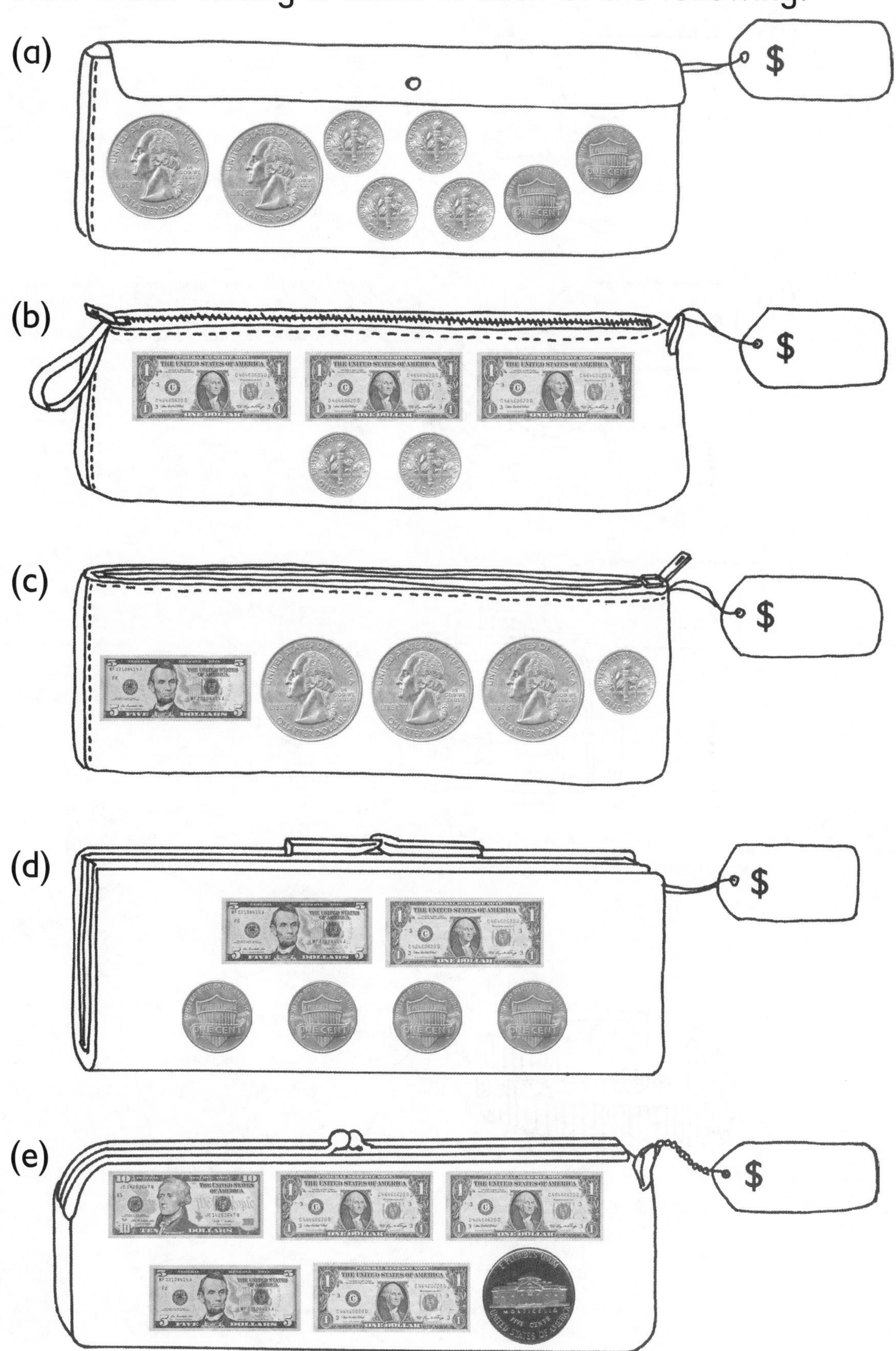

3. What is the cost of each item?

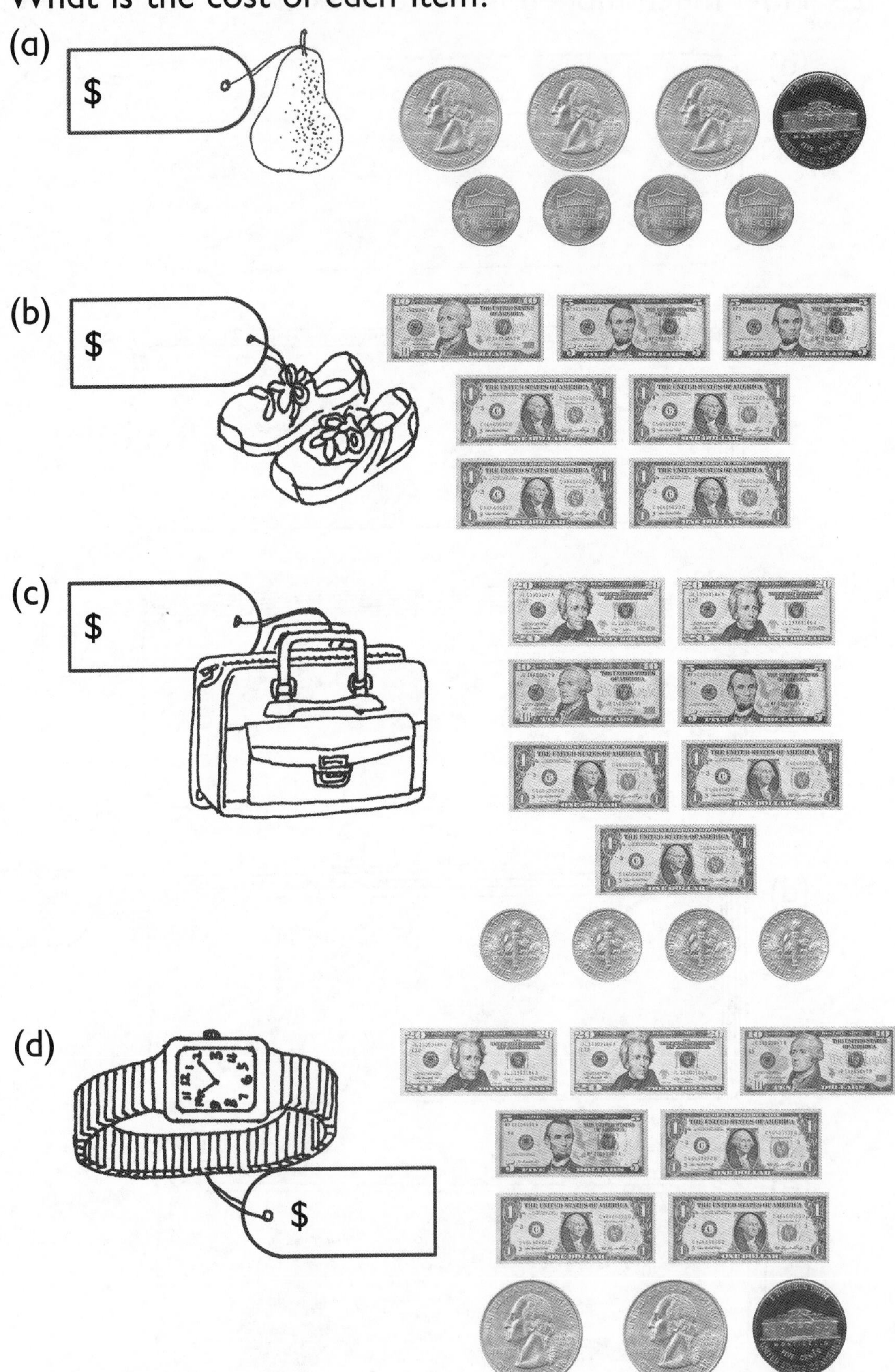

EXERCISE 2

1. Match each amount of money to a coin bank.

5 dollars 45 cents

5 dollars 50 cents

6 dollars 90 cents

9 dollars 60 cents

8 dollars

85 cents

4 dollars 40 cents

4 dollars 5 cents

2. Write each amount of money in figures.

3 dollars 5 cents

4 dollars 30 cents

5 dollars

50 cents

9 dollars 75 cents

9 dollars 90 cents

3. Write the missing numbers.

$6.80 ____ dollars ____ cents

$4.65 ____ dollars ____ cents

$0.70 ____ dollars ____ cents

$6.45 ____ dollars ____ cents

$7.00 ____ dollars ____ cents

4. Match the amounts of money in words with the correct animals.

Twenty-three dollars

Four dollars

Thirteen dollars and thirty cents

Twenty cents

Seven dollars and fifty cents

Ninety-nine dollars and five cents

5. Write each amount of money in figures.

Fifteen cents	$0.15
Twenty dollars	
Forty-seven dollars	
Seventy-four dollars and fifty cents	
Thirty dollars and forty-five cents	
Eighty-six dollars and five cents	
Forty-seven dollars and fifteen cents	
Ninety-five cents	
Ninety-five dollars and five cents	
Forty dollars and twenty-five cents	

EXERCISE 3

1. Match the mice to the cheese.

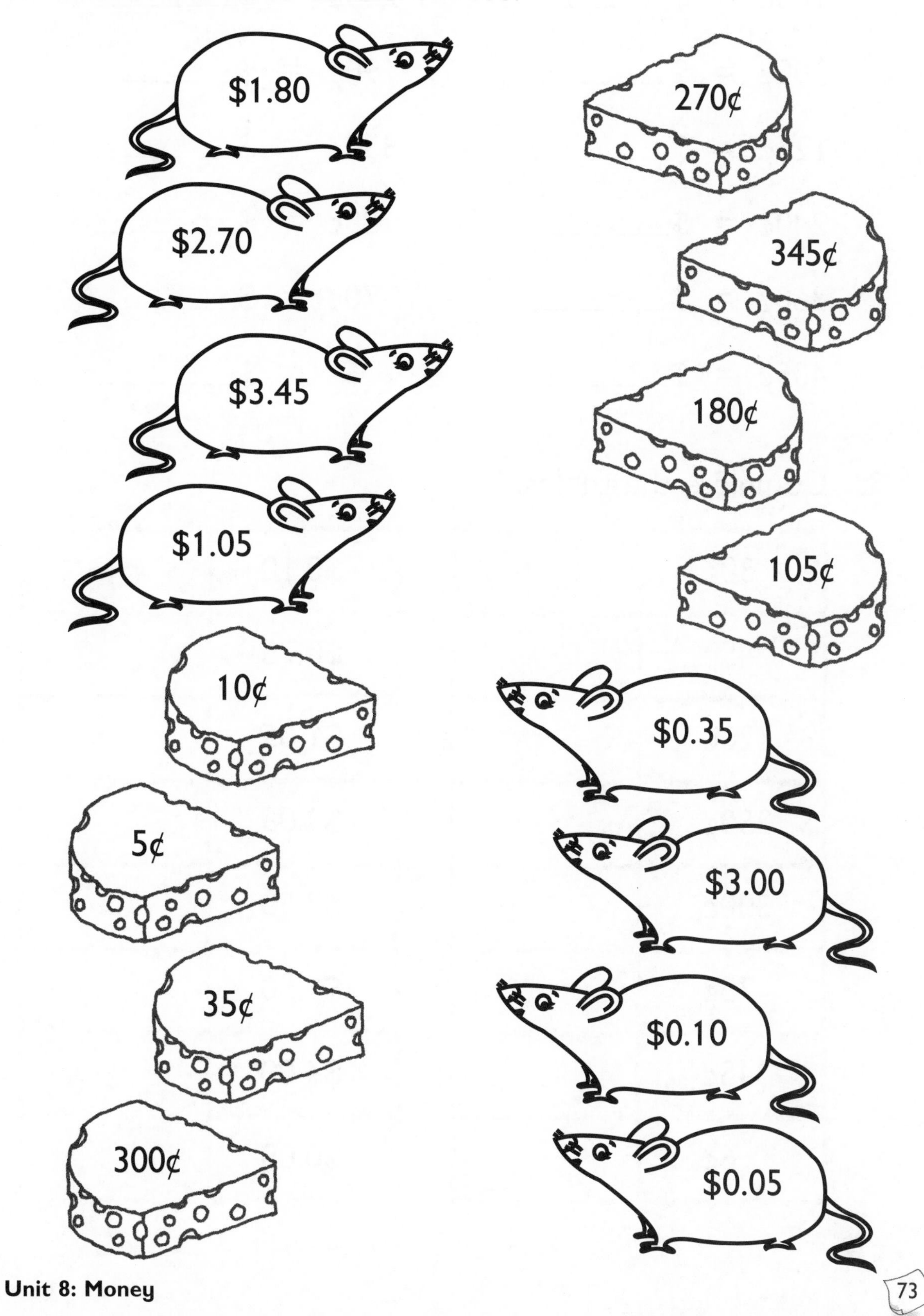

2. Write in dollars.

100¢ = $ 1.00

205¢ = $ ______

200¢ = $ ______

190¢ = $ ______

125¢ = $ ______

350¢ = $ ______

240¢ = $ ______

85¢ = $ ______

360¢ = $ ______

70¢ = $ ______

405¢ = $ ______

5¢ = $ ______

3. Complete the tables.

30¢	$0.30
45¢	
120¢	
250¢	
300¢	
75¢	
345¢	
6¢	

$0.10	10¢
$0.75	
$1.05	
$3.05	
$7.50	
$1.50	
$4.00	
$0.08	

EXERCISE 4

1. How much money is needed to make $1?

(a)

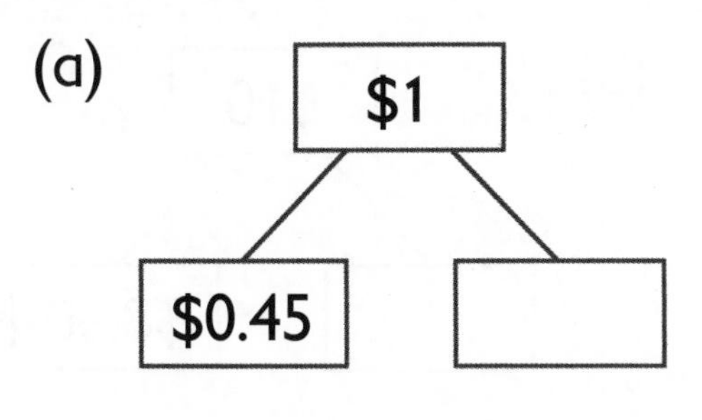

(b)

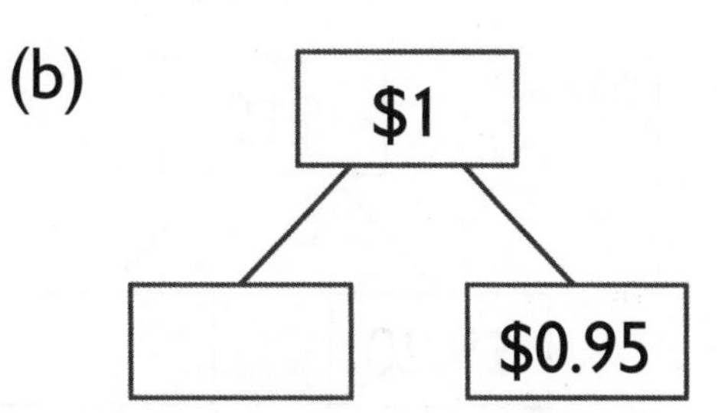

(c)

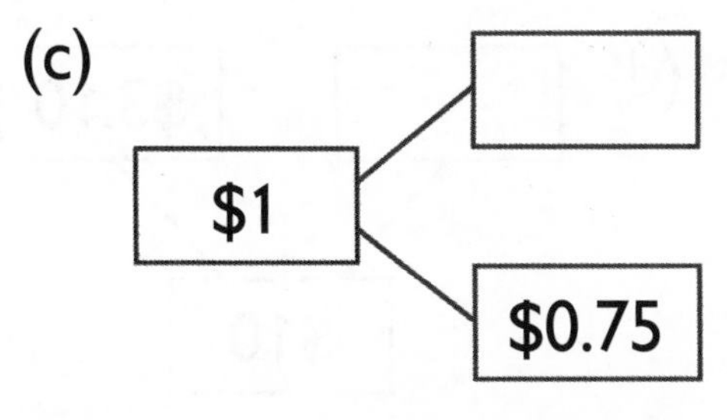

(d)

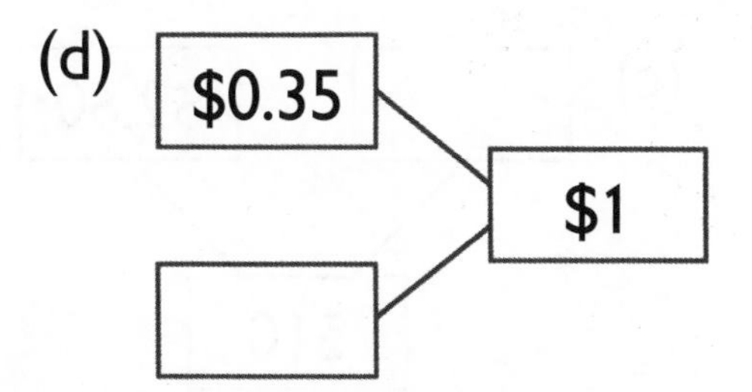

2. Write the missing amount of money on each arrow.

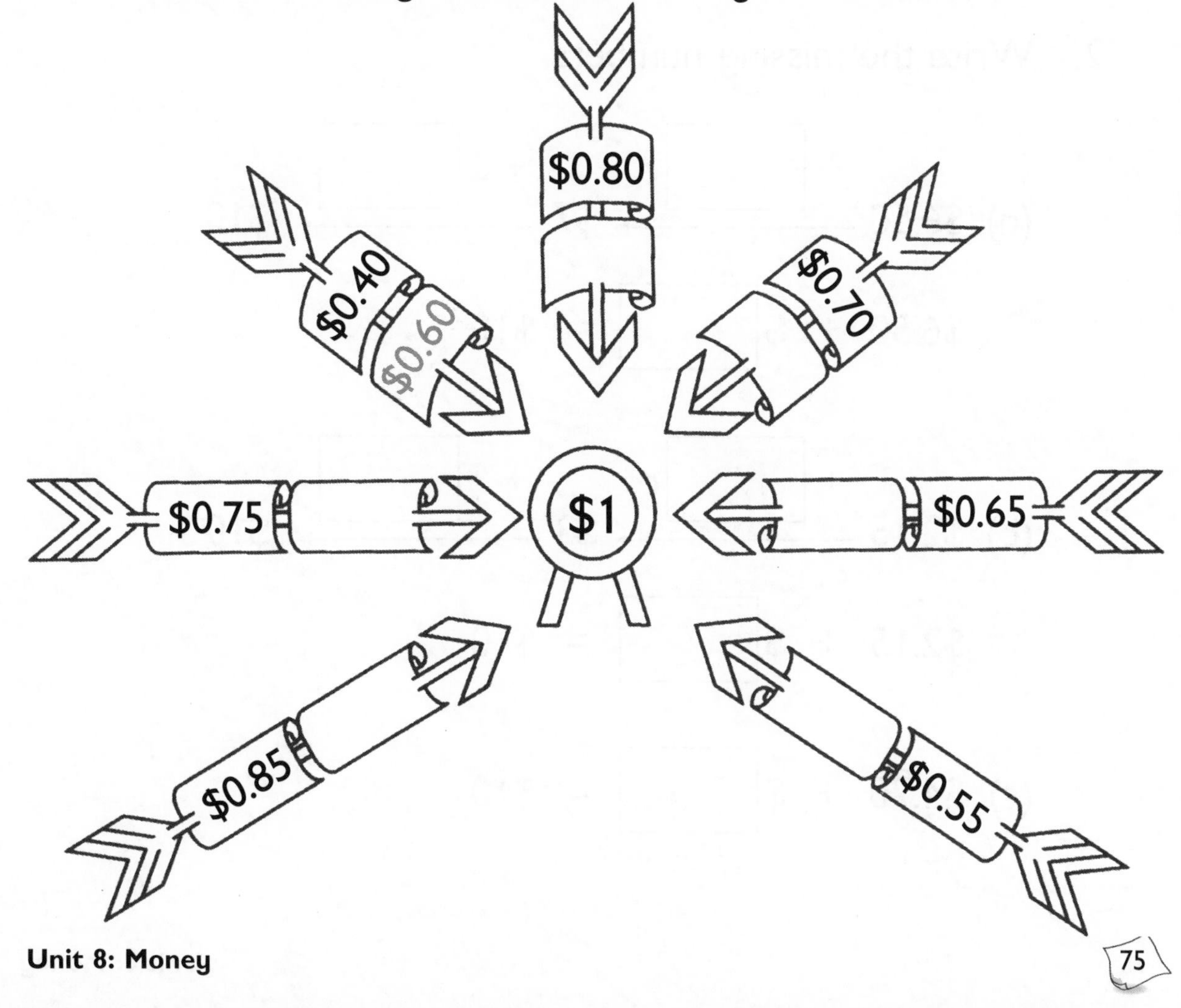

EXERCISE 5

1. How much money is needed to make $10?

(a)

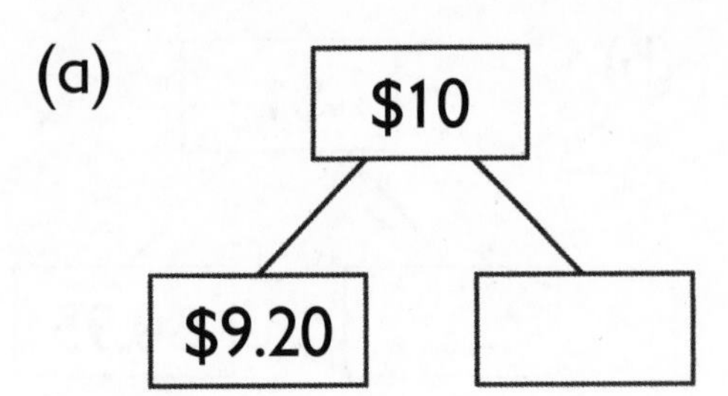

(b)

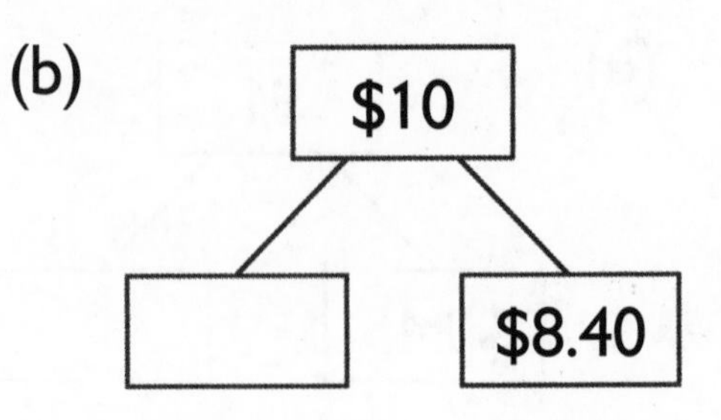

(c)

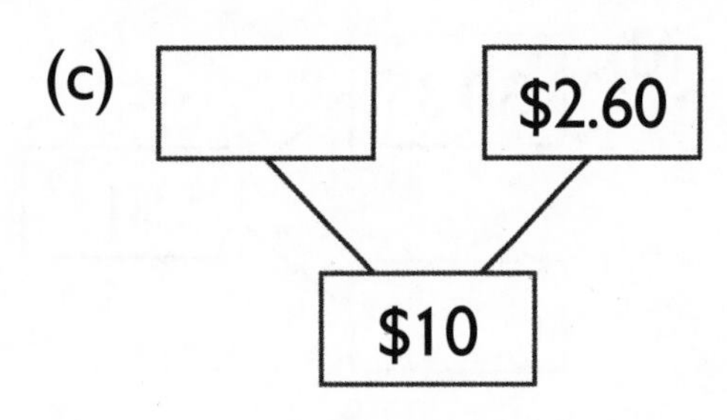

(d)

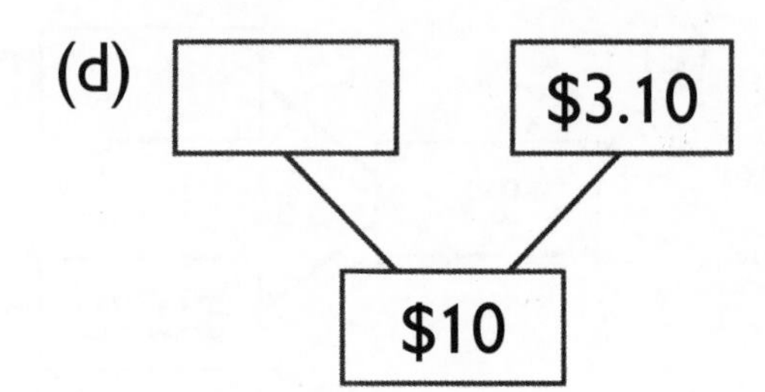

2. Write the missing numbers.

(a) $6.50 —(+ ☐ ¢)→ $7 —(+ $ ☐)→ $10

$6.50 + $ ☐ = $10

(b) $2.15 —(+ ☐ ¢)→ $3 —(+ $ ☐)→ $10

$2.15 + $ ☐ = $10

(c) $4.70 + $ ☐ = $10

3. Hassan bought this pencil sharpener.
He gave the cashier $1.
How much change did he receive?

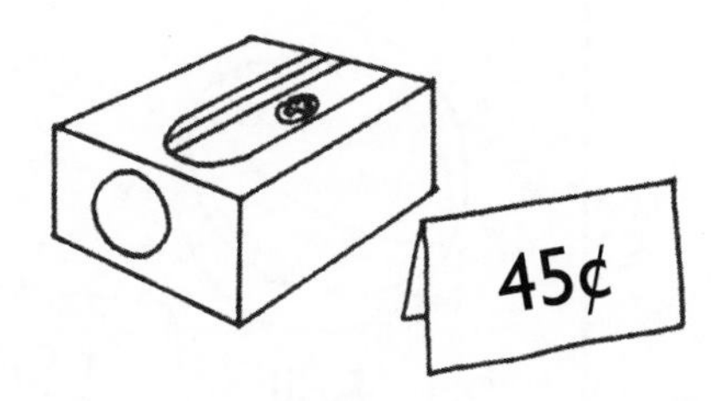

4. Mai had $10.
She bought this vase.
How much money did she have left?

5.

(a) Amy bought the ball and the ruler.
How much did she spend altogether?

(b) Haley had $1.
She bought the pen.
How much money did she have left?

(c) Larry bought the jigsaw puzzle.
He gave the cashier $10.
How much change did he receive?

(d) How much cheaper is the flying saucer than the book?

(e) Matthew bought 2 of the items.
He spent $10 altogether.
Which items did he buy?

EXERCISE 6

1. Add.

(a) $0.85 —(+ $4)→ $ ☐

(b) $1.45 —(+ $3)→ $ ☐

(c) $2.05 —(+ $8)→ $ ☐

(d) $3.70 —(+ $10)→ $ ☐

(e) $2.35 —(+ 20¢)→ $ ☐

(f) $1.25 —(+ 65¢)→ $ ☐

(g) $2.60 —(+ 15¢)→ $ ☐

(h) $3.75 —(+ 5¢)→ $ ☐

(i) $3.40 —(+ 60¢)→ $ ☐

(j) $2.75 —(+ 25¢)→ $ ☐

(k) $4.35 —(+ 65¢)→ $ ☐

(l) $4.45 —(+ 55¢)→ $ ☐

EXERCISE 7

1. Write the missing numbers.

(a) $1.45 —+ $2→ $ ☐ —+ 30¢→ $ ☐

$1.45 + $2.30 = $ ☐

(b) $2.60 —+ $3→ $ ☐ —+ 25¢→ $ ☐

$2.60 + $3.25 = $ ☐

(c) $3.15 —+ $2→ $ ☐ —+ 65¢→ $ ☐

$3.15 + $2.65 = $ ☐

2. Add.

(a) $2.40 + $1.20 =
(b) $4.20 + $2.70 =
(c) $2.55 + $2.35 =
(d) $3.75 + $1.05 =
(e) $2.45 + $3.15 =
(f) $6.25 + $2.65 =

EXERCISE 8

1. Add.

$0.85 + $2.20 = ___ E	$3.60 + $1.85 = ___ F	$2.75 + $0.80 = ___ L
$7.75 + $0.60 = ___ N	$4.15 + $3.95 = ___ O	$5.25 + $3.95 = ___ R
$4.45 + $1.75 = ___ S	$2.95 + $3.05 = ___ U	$1.55 + $7.55 = ___ W

What is the name of this flower?

Write the letters in the boxes below to find out.

							E	
$6.20	$6.00	$8.35	$5.45	$3.55	$8.10	$9.10	$3.05	$9.20

EXERCISE 9

1. Add.

(a) \$2.45 + \$0.99 =
(b) \$4.15 + \$3.99 =
(c) \$3.55 + \$1.99 =
(d) \$3.25 + \$2.99 =

2. Add.

(a) \$3.80 + \$0.95 =
(b) \$2.65 + \$0.95 =
(c) \$3.40 + \$2.95 =
(d) \$4.35 + \$3.95 =

EXERCISE 10

1. Molly bought a ball for $2.40.
   She also bought a toy airplane for $3.25.
   How much did she spend altogether?

---

2. Peter bought a game for $5.98.
   He had $1.22 left.
   How much money did he have at first?

---

3. Paula bought a snack from a vending machine for 65¢.
   Later, she bought lunch for $3.45.
   How much did she spend on food?

4. Sally has $4.50.
   Her brother has $2.35 more.
   How much money does her brother have?

5. Carlie gets an allowance of $3 a week.
   She saves $2.45 the first week and 95¢ the second week.
   The third week, she saves all her allowance.
   How much money does she save altogether?

6. Matthew counted his money.
   He had 2 twenty-dollar bills, 3 five-dollar bills, 6 one-dollar bills, 8 quarters, 4 dimes, 3 nickels, and 18 pennies.
   How much money did he have altogether?

EXERCISE 11

1. Subtract.

(a)	$4.85	– $3 →	$ ☐
(b)	$6.45	– $2 →	$ ☐
(c)	$7.05	– $4 →	$ ☐
(d)	$9.25	– $8 →	$ ☐
(e)	$2.95	– 60¢ →	$ ☐
(f)	$5.75	– 70¢ →	$ ☐
(g)	$6.40	– 40¢ →	$ ☐
(h)	$9.80	– 65¢ →	$ ☐
(i)	$4	– 80¢ →	$ ☐
(j)	$5	– 70¢ →	$ ☐
(k)	$3	– 55¢ →	$ ☐
(l)	$6	– 75¢ →	$ ☐

EXERCISE 12

1. Write the missing numbers.

(a) $6.80 $\xrightarrow{-\ \$2}$ $ ☐ $\xrightarrow{-\ 50¢}$ $ ☐

$6.80 – $2.50 = $ ☐

(b) $4.75 $\xrightarrow{-\ \$3}$ $ ☐ $\xrightarrow{-\ 35¢}$ $ ☐

$4.75 – $3.35 = $ ☐

(c) $5.90 $\xrightarrow{-\ \$3}$ $ ☐ $\xrightarrow{-\ 65¢}$ $ ☐

$5.90 – $3.65 = $ ☐

2. Subtract.

(a) $4.80 – $1.20 =
(b) $5.85 – $2.60 =
(c) $5.90 – $3.75 =
(d) $6.70 – $2.35 =
(e) $4.50 – $2.05 =
(f) $7.70 – $3.45 =

EXERCISE 13

1. Subtract.

$2.25 − $0.60 A	$3.10 − $0.55 D	$5.00 − $0.25 F
$7.00 − $4.70 G	$6.35 − $3.50 L	$7.05 − $2.45 N
$8.50 − $5.90 O	$4.30 − $3.85 R	$9.20 − $7.65 Y

What is the name of this insect?

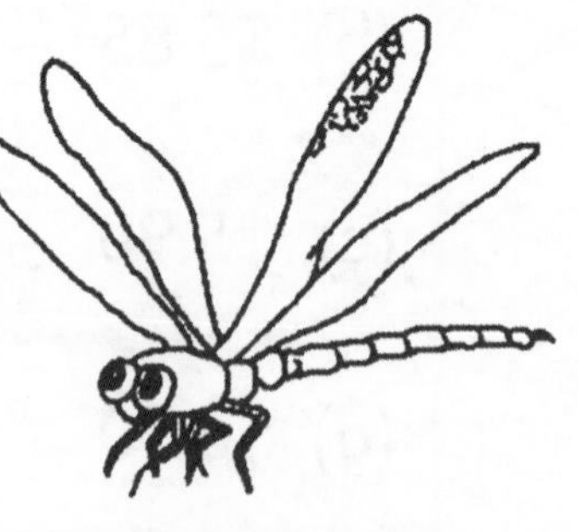

Write the letters in the boxes below to find out.

		A						
$2.55	$0.45	$1.65	$2.30	$2.60	$4.60	$4.75	$2.85	$1.55

EXERCISE 14

1. Subtract.

(a) $4.30 – $0.99 =
(b) $3.45 – $0.99 =
(c) $4.25 – $1.99 =
(d) $6.00 – $2.99 =

2. Subtract.

(a) $2.20 – $0.95 =
(b) $3.55 – $0.95 =
(c) $4.10 – $3.95 =
(d) $8.25 – $5.95 =

EXERCISE 15

1. Ben bought a snack that cost 55¢ from a vending machine.
   He put a one-dollar bill into the machine.
   How much change did he get?

2. Sam had $8.
   He bought a toy car for $5.35.
   How much money did he have left?

3. A toy robot costs $5.90.
   A doll costs $3.85.
   How much cheaper is the doll?

4. Sara bought this set of stamps from a post office.
   She had $6.30 left.
   How much money did she have at first?

---

5. Miguel spent $2.60 on his lunch.
   His brother spent $0.95 more than he.
   How much did his brother spend?

---

6. Lily saved $10.
   She saved $1.95 more than Jose.
   How much did Jose save?

REVIEW 8

1. Write the price of each object in words.

(a) $5.90 ______________________________

(b) $9.50 ______________________________

(c) 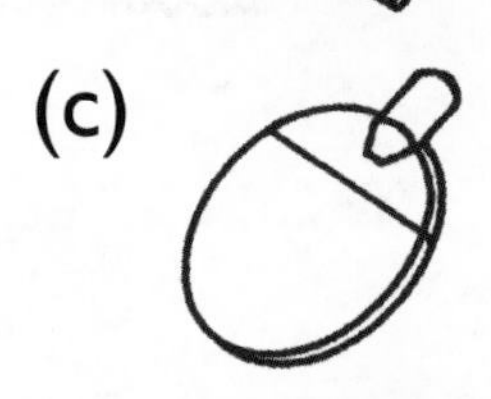

$5.09 ______________________________

(d) 

$9.05 ______________________________

2. Add or subtract.

(a) \$3.65 + \$6.30 =	(b) \$7.20 – \$4.60 =
(c) \$3.85 + \$2.05 =	(d) \$4.25 – \$1.45 =
(e) \$4.55 + \$0.99 =	(f) \$10 – \$2.95 =

3. Juanita bought a key chain for $3.95.
She gave the cashier $10.
How much change did she receive?

4.

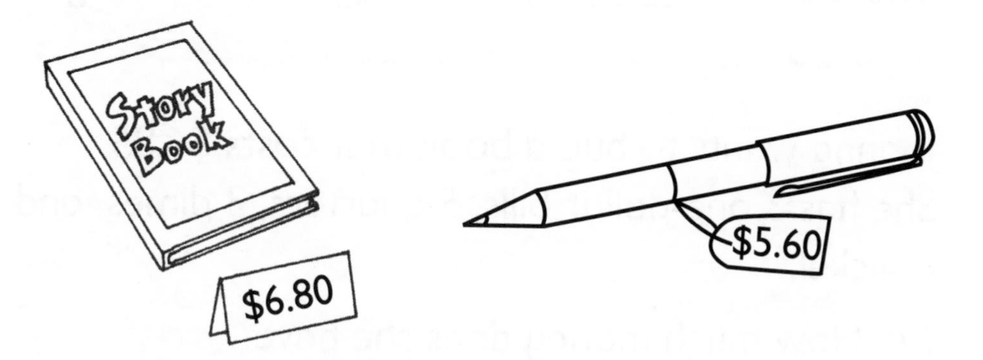

(a) Kevin bought the book and the pen.
How much did he spend altogether?

(b) After buying the book and the pen, Kevin had $15 left.
How much money did he have at first?

5.

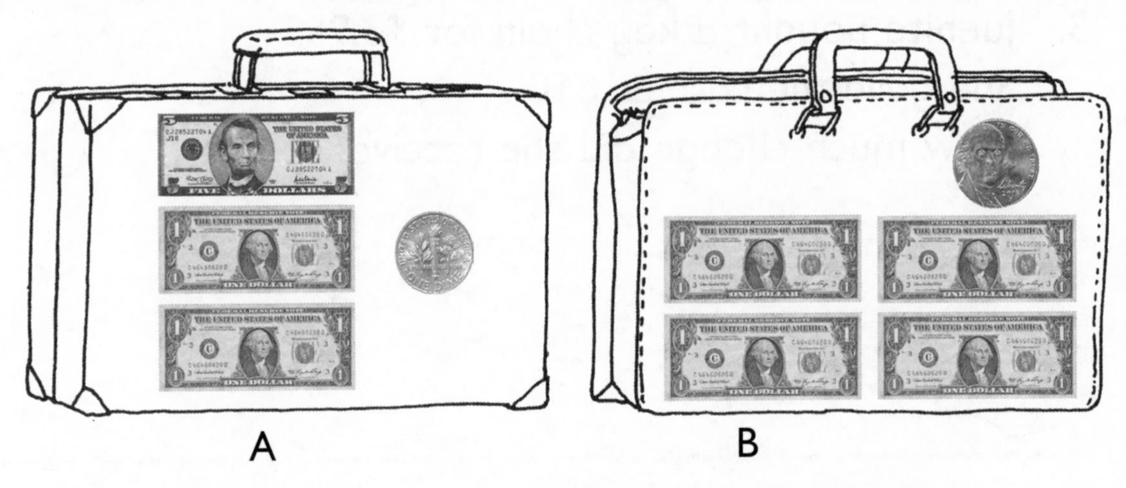

There is $________ more in Bag A than in Bag B.

6. Joanna wants to buy a book that costs $6.85.
She has 3 one-dollar bills, 5 quarters, 3 dimes, and a nickel.

(a) How much money does she have?

(b) How much more money does she need?

7. Sarina, Sue, Rosa, and Molly spent $36 on lunch.
They shared the cost equally.
How much did each of them pay?

8. Cameron bought 6 T-shirts.
How much did he pay altogether?

9. A calculator costs $9.50.
A pen is $1.60 cheaper than the calculator.
Find the cost of the pen.

10. 10 dolls cost \$70.
Find the cost of 1 doll.

11. Mike bought 20 apples at 4 for \$1.
How much did he pay?

12. A magazine costs \$3.80.
A book costs 2 quarters more than the magazine.
Find the cost of the book.

13. A toy costs $6.05.
Ryan has 24 quarters and 2 nickels.
Does he have enough money to buy the toy?

---

14. Andy bought an eraser for 29 cents.
He gave the cashier 2 quarters.
How much change did he receive?

---

15. Bonita has 32 quarters, 12 dimes, 6 nickels, and 3 pennies.
How much money does she have?

EXERCISE 1

1. Check (✓) the pictures that show $\frac{1}{2}$.

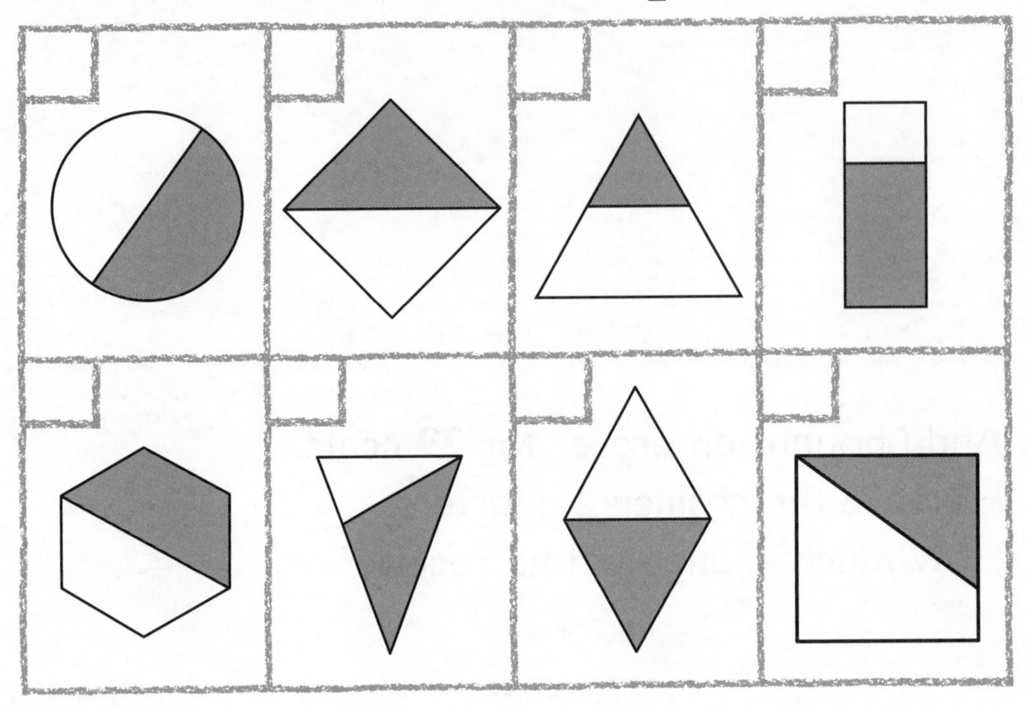

2. Check (✓) the pictures that show $\frac{1}{4}$.

3. Check (✓) the pictures that show $\frac{1}{2}$.

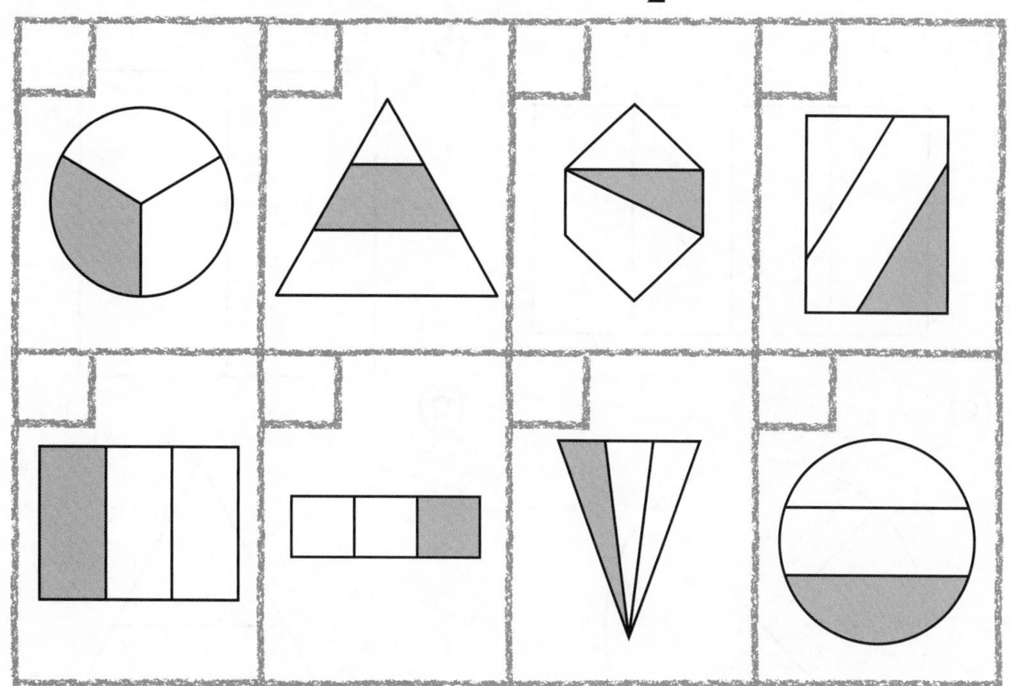

4. Color $\frac{1}{2}$ of each shape.

(a)

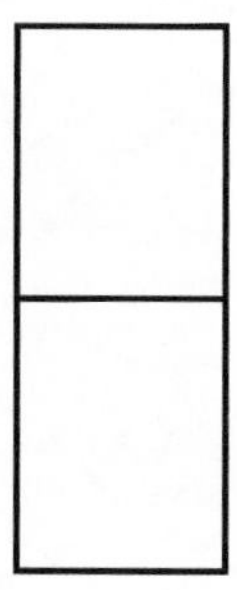

(b)

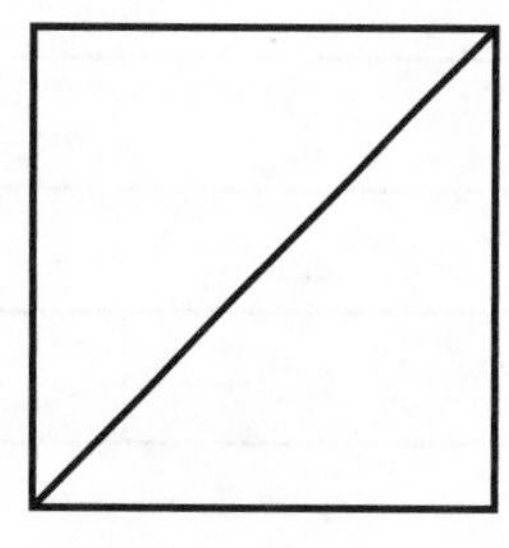

(c)

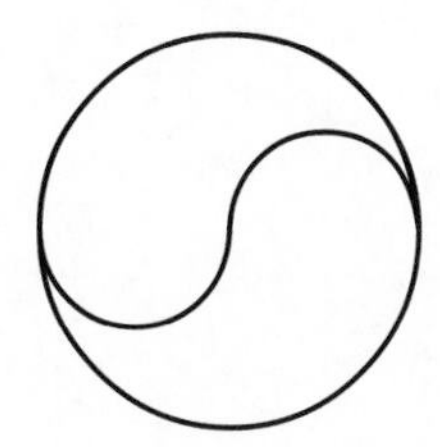

(d)

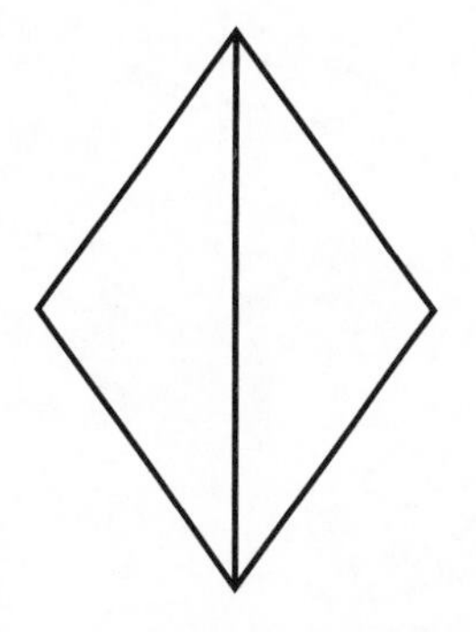

5. Color $\frac{1}{4}$ of each shape.

(a)

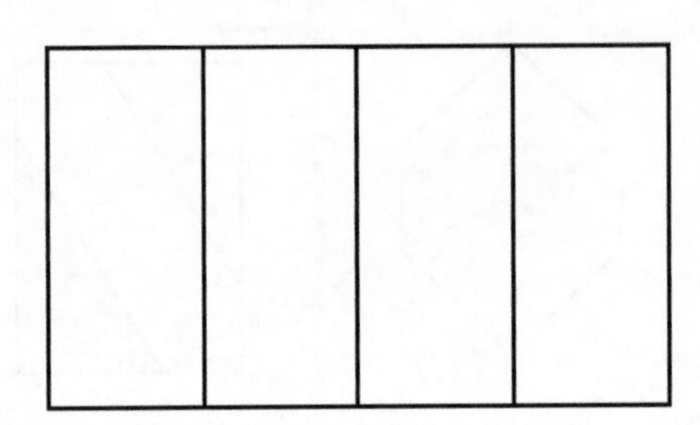

(b)

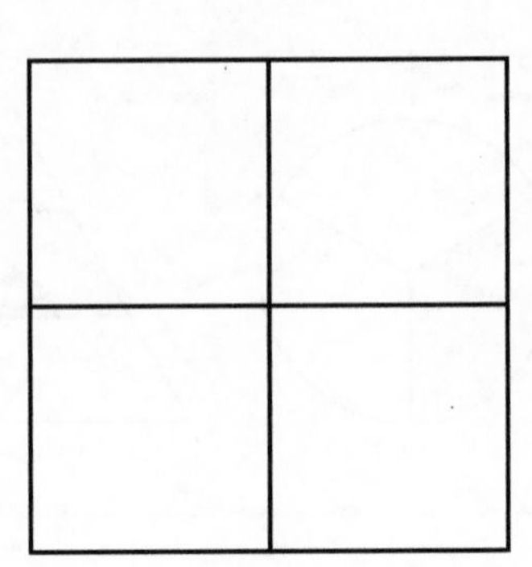

(c)

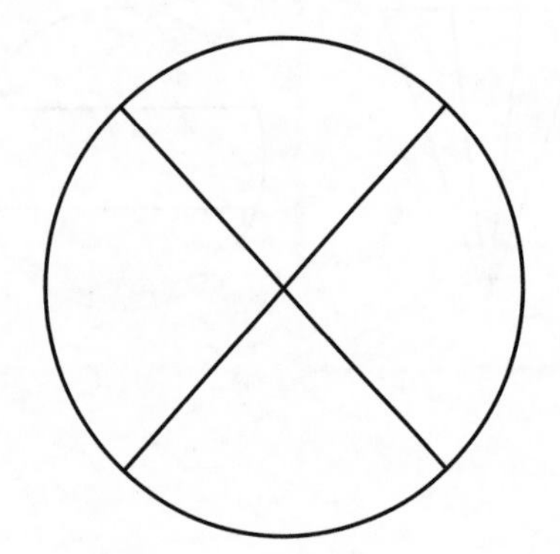

(d)

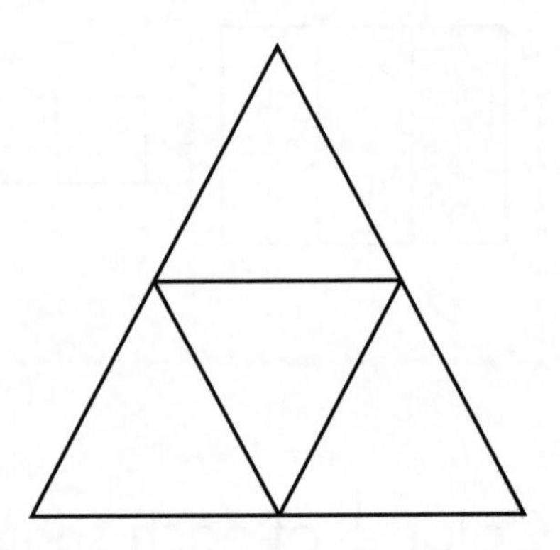

6. Color to show the fraction.

(a) $\frac{1}{2}$

(b) $\frac{1}{3}$

(c) $\frac{1}{4}$

7. Fill in the blanks.

(a) 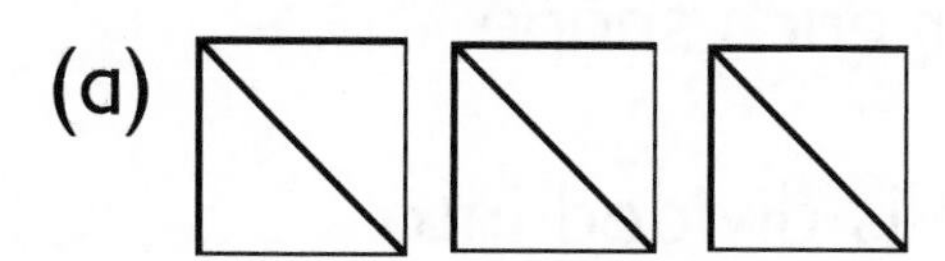

How many halves are there in 3 wholes? ________

(b) 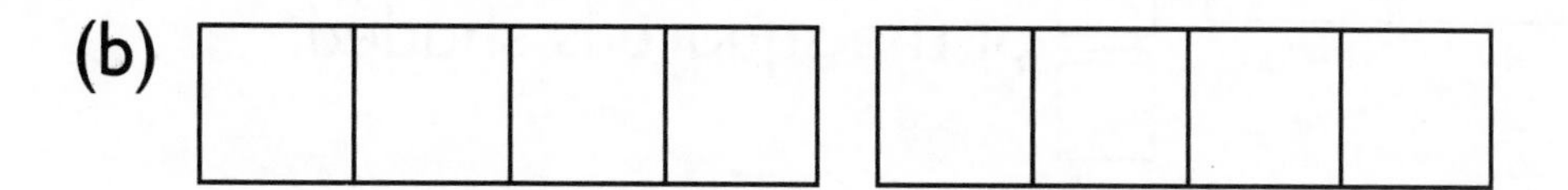

How many fourths are there in 2 wholes? ________

(c) 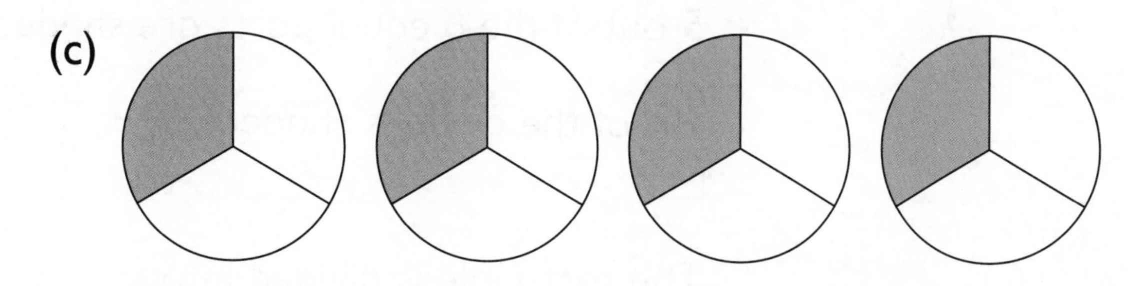

How many thirds are there in 4 wholes? ________

EXERCISE 2

1. Write the correct fraction for each shape.

(a) The square is divided into 3 equal parts.
2 out of the 3 equal parts are shaded.
☐/☐ of the square is shaded.

(b) The circle is divided into 8 equal parts.
5 out of the 8 equal parts are shaded.
☐/☐ of the circle is shaded.

(c) The rectangle is divided into 10 equal parts.
7 out of the 10 equal parts are shaded.
☐/☐ of the rectangle is shaded.

(d) The triangle is divided into 4 equal parts.
3 out of the 4 equal parts are shaded.
☐/☐ of the triangle is shaded.

2. (a)

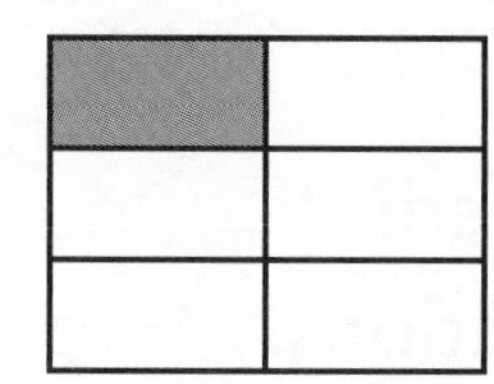

$\frac{1}{6}$ of the shape is shaded.

$\frac{1}{6}$ is ☐ out of the ☐ equal parts.

(b)

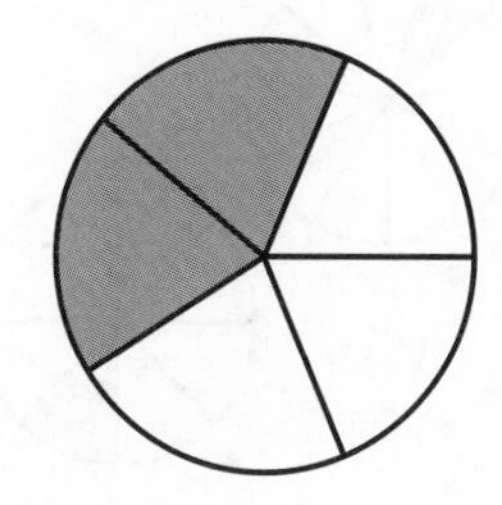

$\frac{2}{5}$ of the shape is shaded.

$\frac{2}{5}$ is ☐ out of the ☐ equal parts.

(c)

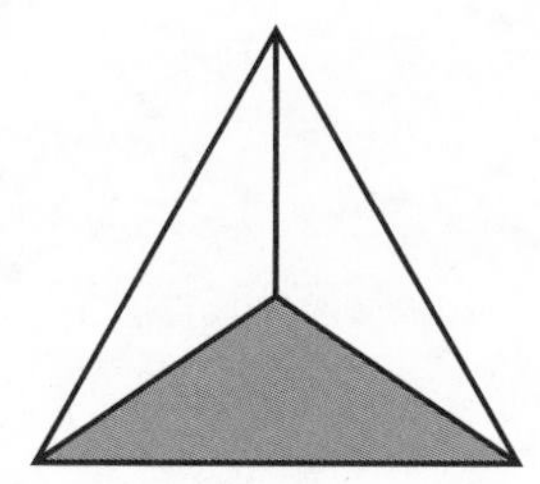

$\frac{1}{3}$ of the shape is shaded.

$\frac{1}{3}$ is ☐ out of the ☐ equal parts.

(d)

$\frac{3}{4}$ of the shape is shaded.

$\frac{3}{4}$ is ☐ out of the ☐ equal parts.

(e)

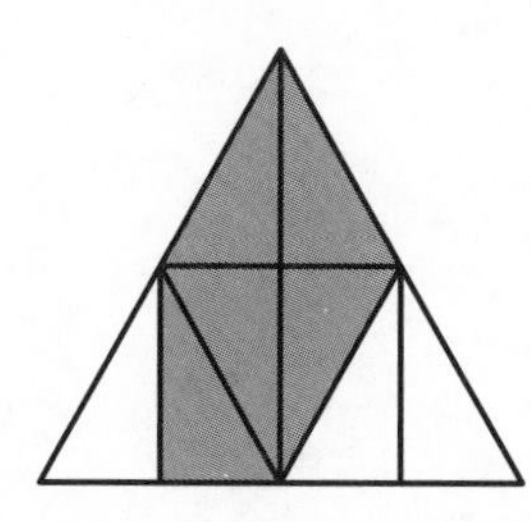

$\frac{5}{8}$ of the shape is shaded.

$\frac{5}{8}$ is ☐ out of the ☐ equal parts.

EXERCISE 3

1. What fraction of each circle is shaded?
   Match the circles to the correct fractions.

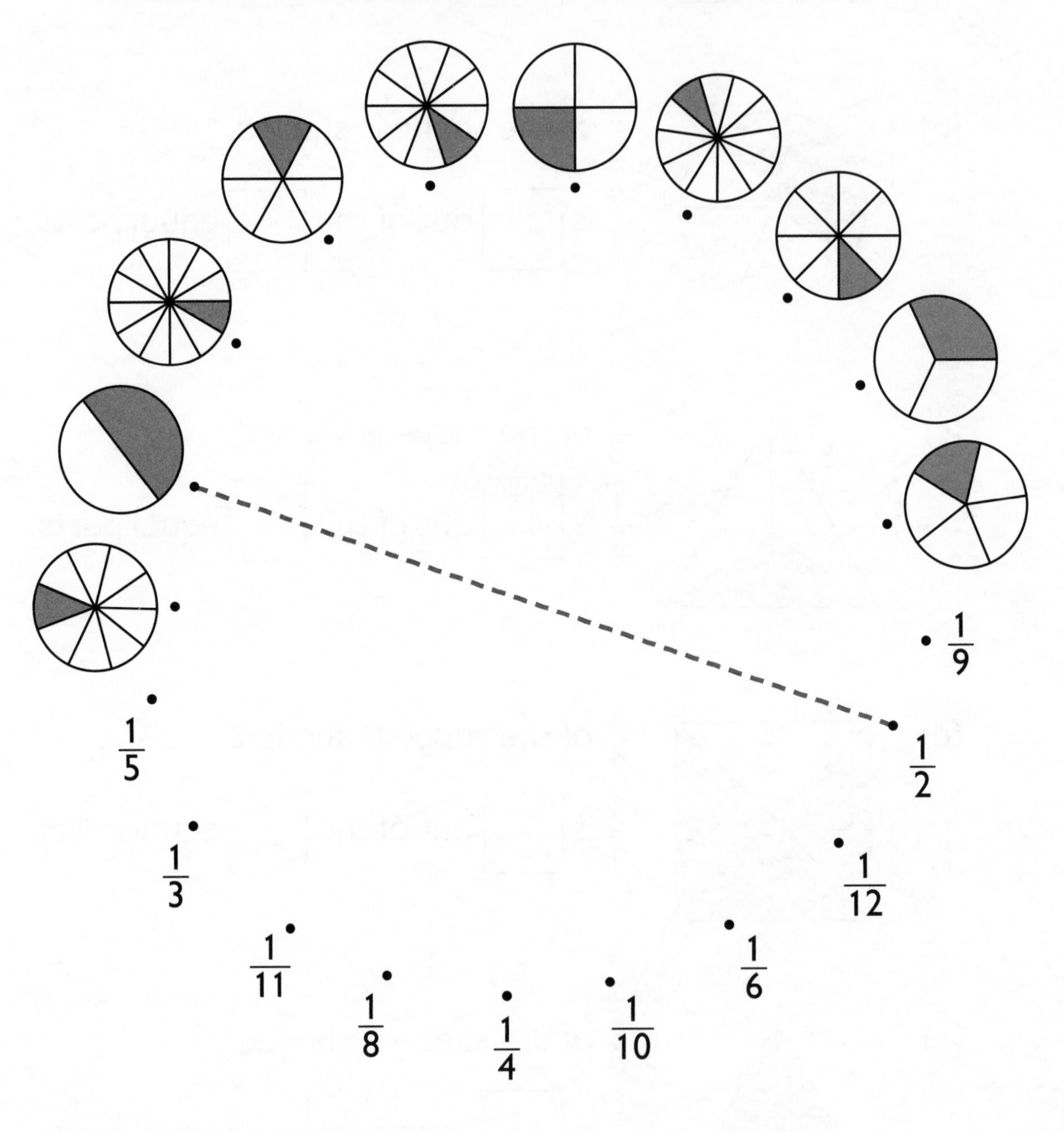

2. What fraction of each shape is shaded?
Match the shapes to the correct fractions.

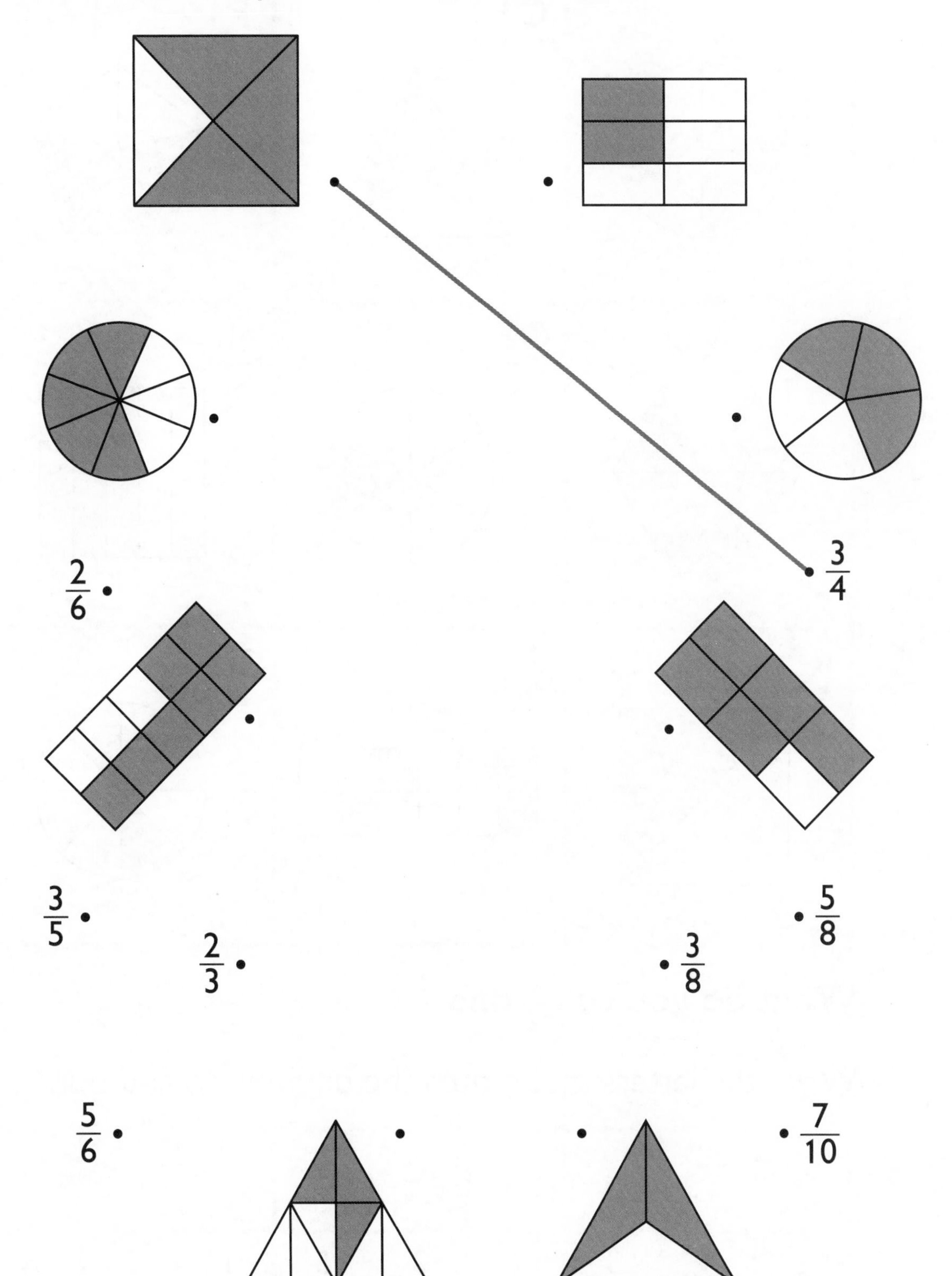

3. What fraction of each shape is shaded?

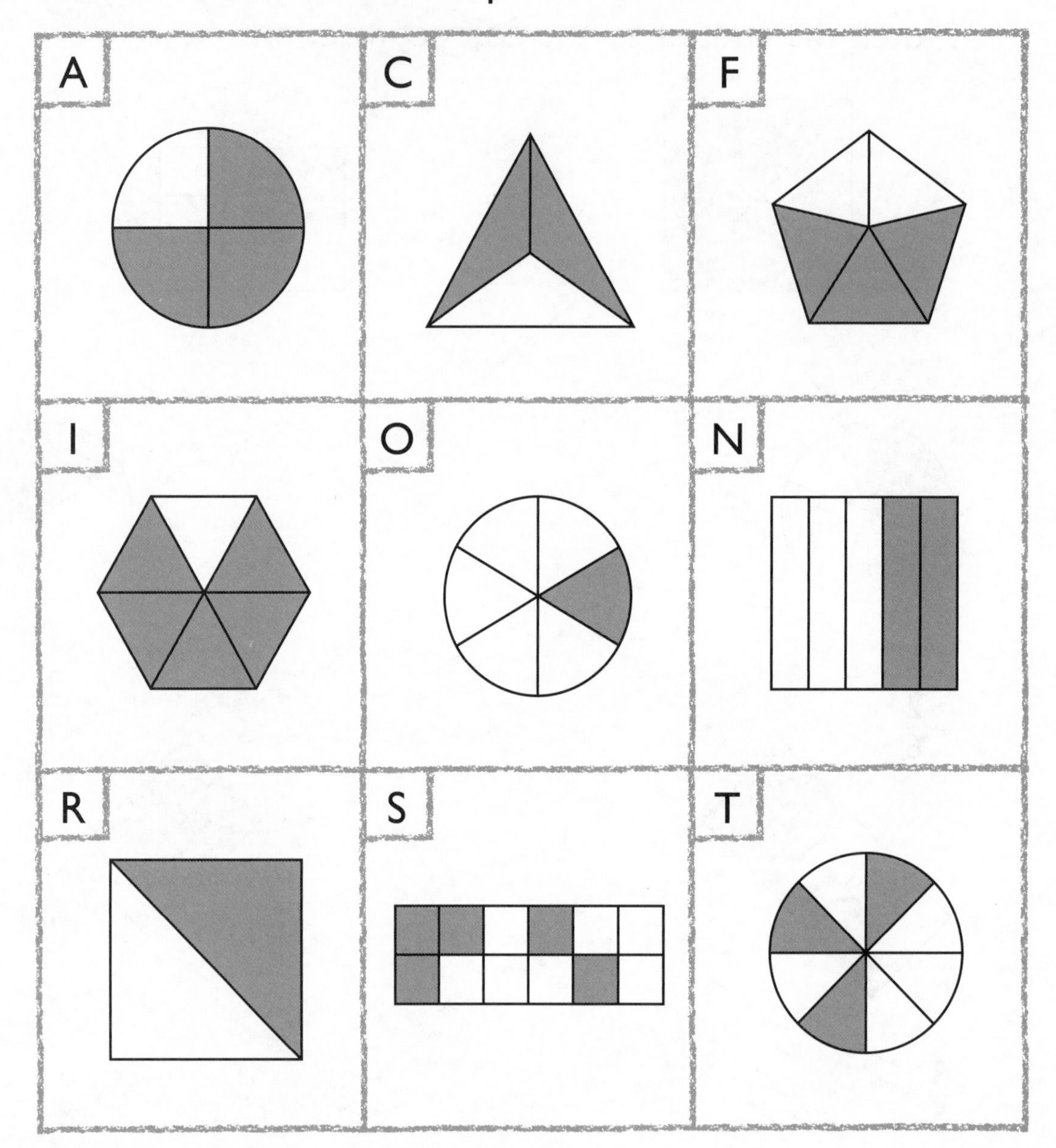

What do you call $\frac{1}{2}$ and $\frac{1}{4}$?

Write the letters that match the answers to find out.

		A						
$\frac{3}{5}$	$\frac{1}{2}$	$\frac{3}{4}$	$\frac{2}{3}$	$\frac{3}{8}$	$\frac{5}{6}$	$\frac{1}{6}$	$\frac{2}{5}$	$\frac{5}{12}$

4. Color to show each given fraction.

$\frac{1}{4}$ 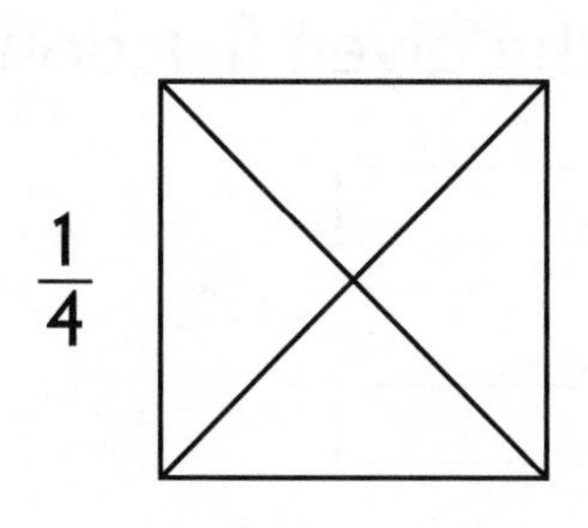

$\frac{1}{2}$ 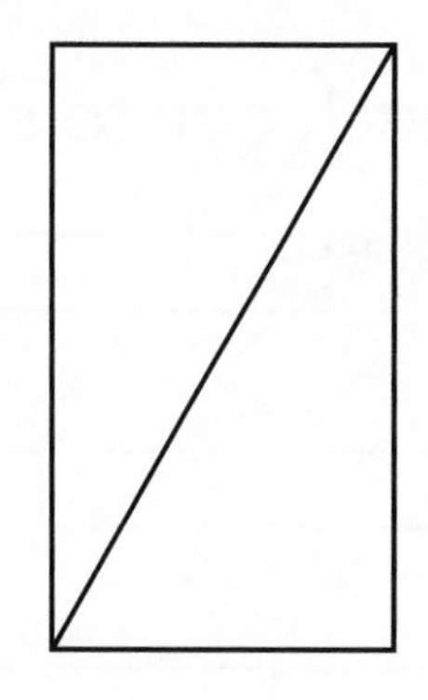

$\frac{2}{3}$ 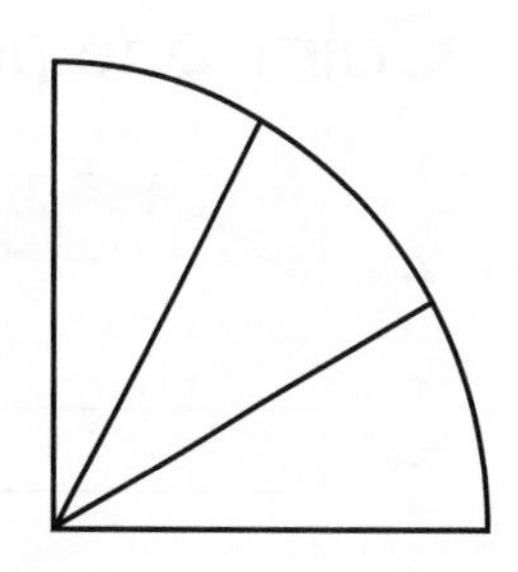

$\frac{3}{8}$

$\frac{7}{8}$ 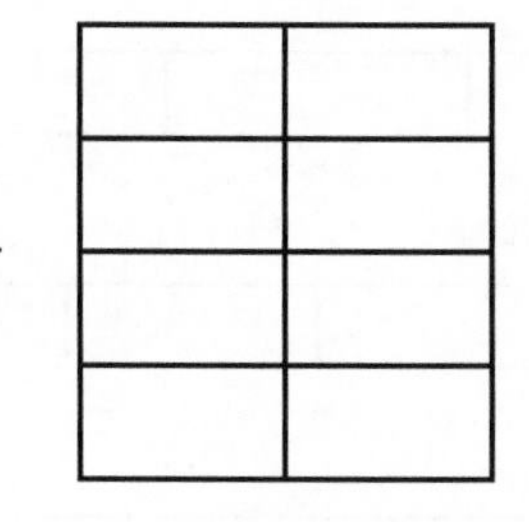

$\frac{4}{5}$ 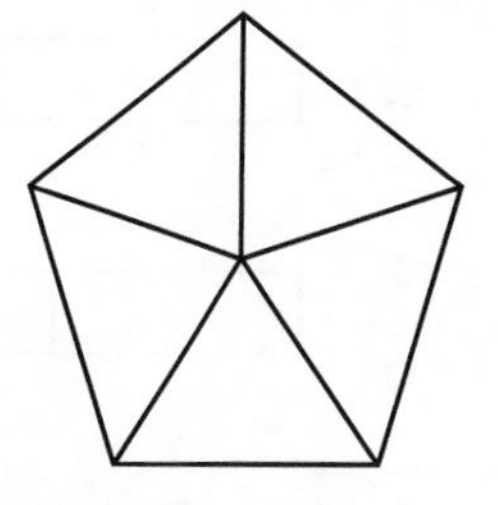

$\frac{2}{10}$ 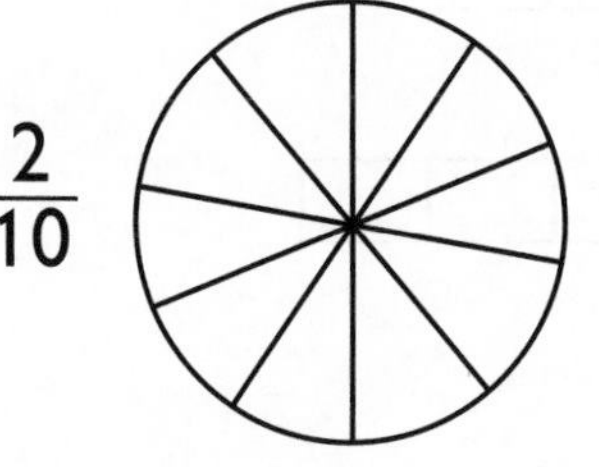

$\frac{5}{6}$ 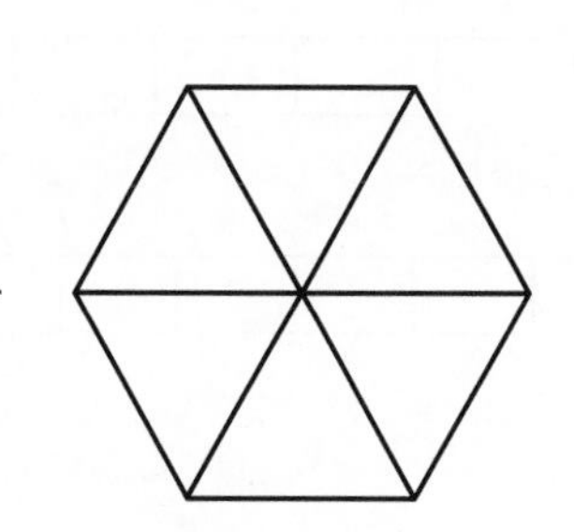

$\frac{3}{4}$ 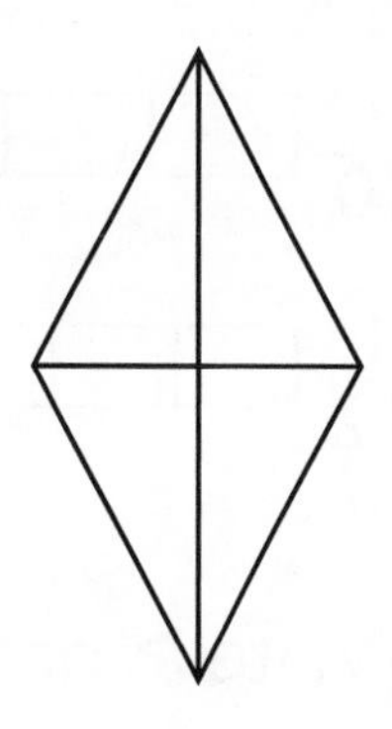

$\frac{2}{5}$ 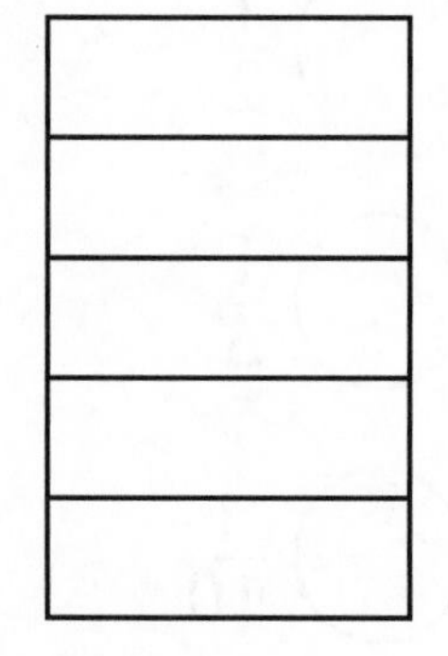

$\frac{3}{6}$ 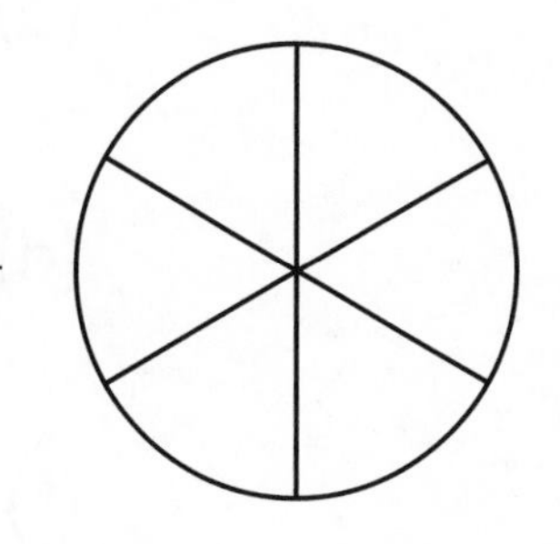

$\frac{9}{10}$ 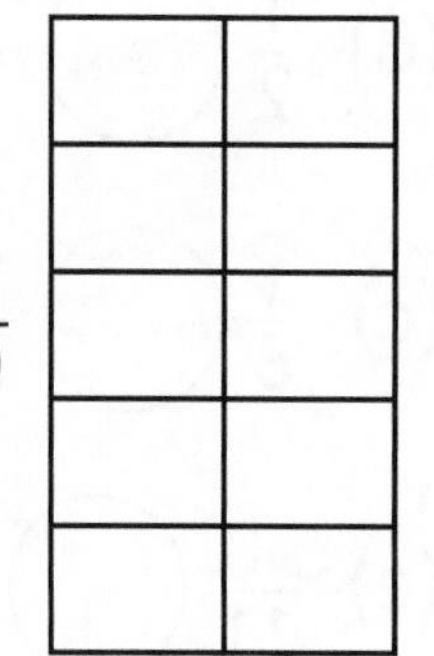

EXERCISE 4

1. Color one part of each bar to show the given fraction.

$\frac{1}{2}$

$\frac{1}{3}$

$\frac{1}{4}$

$\frac{1}{5}$

$\frac{1}{6}$

$\frac{1}{8}$

$\frac{1}{10}$

$\frac{1}{12}$

2. Write > or <.
(Use the fraction bars above to help you.)

(a) $\frac{1}{2} \bigcirc \frac{1}{3}$

(b) $\frac{1}{6} \bigcirc \frac{1}{2}$

(c) $\frac{1}{8} \bigcirc \frac{1}{2}$

(d) $\frac{1}{3} \bigcirc \frac{1}{6}$

(e) $\frac{1}{11} \bigcirc \frac{1}{2}$

(f) $\frac{1}{5} \bigcirc \frac{1}{10}$

3. Circle the greater fraction.

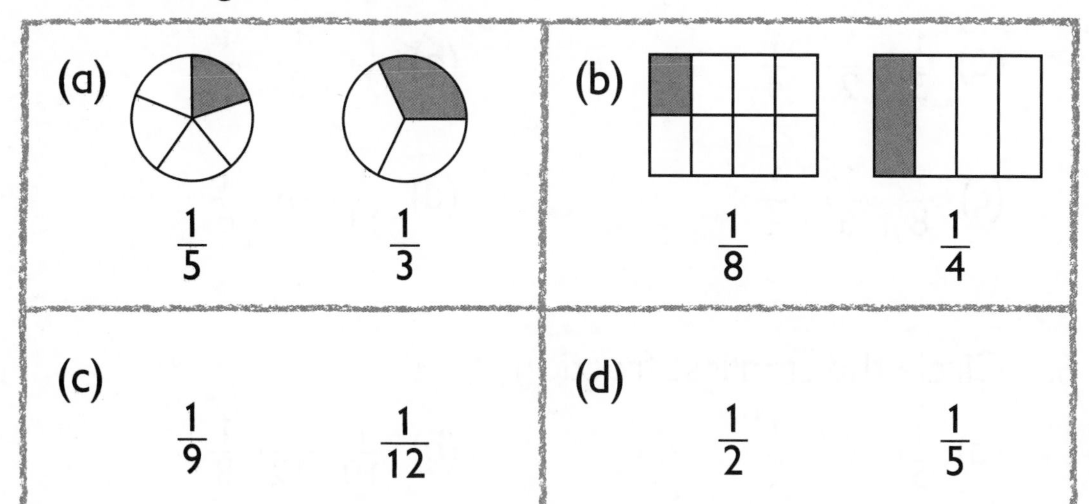

(a) $\frac{1}{5}$ $\frac{1}{3}$

(b) $\frac{1}{8}$ $\frac{1}{4}$

(c) $\frac{1}{9}$ $\frac{1}{12}$

(d) $\frac{1}{2}$ $\frac{1}{5}$

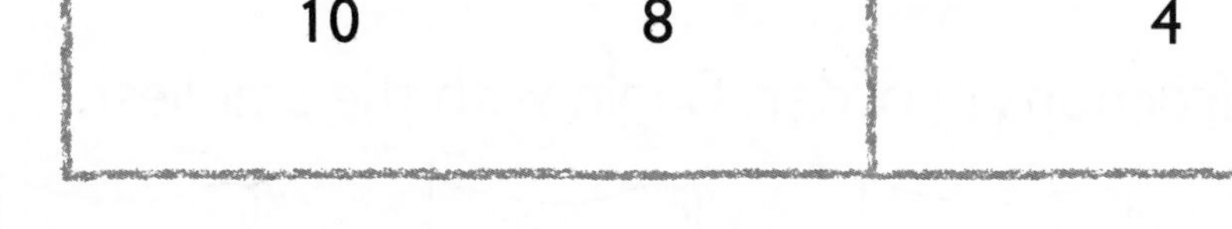

(e) $\frac{1}{10}$ $\frac{1}{8}$

(f) $\frac{1}{4}$ $\frac{1}{6}$

4. Circle the smaller fraction.

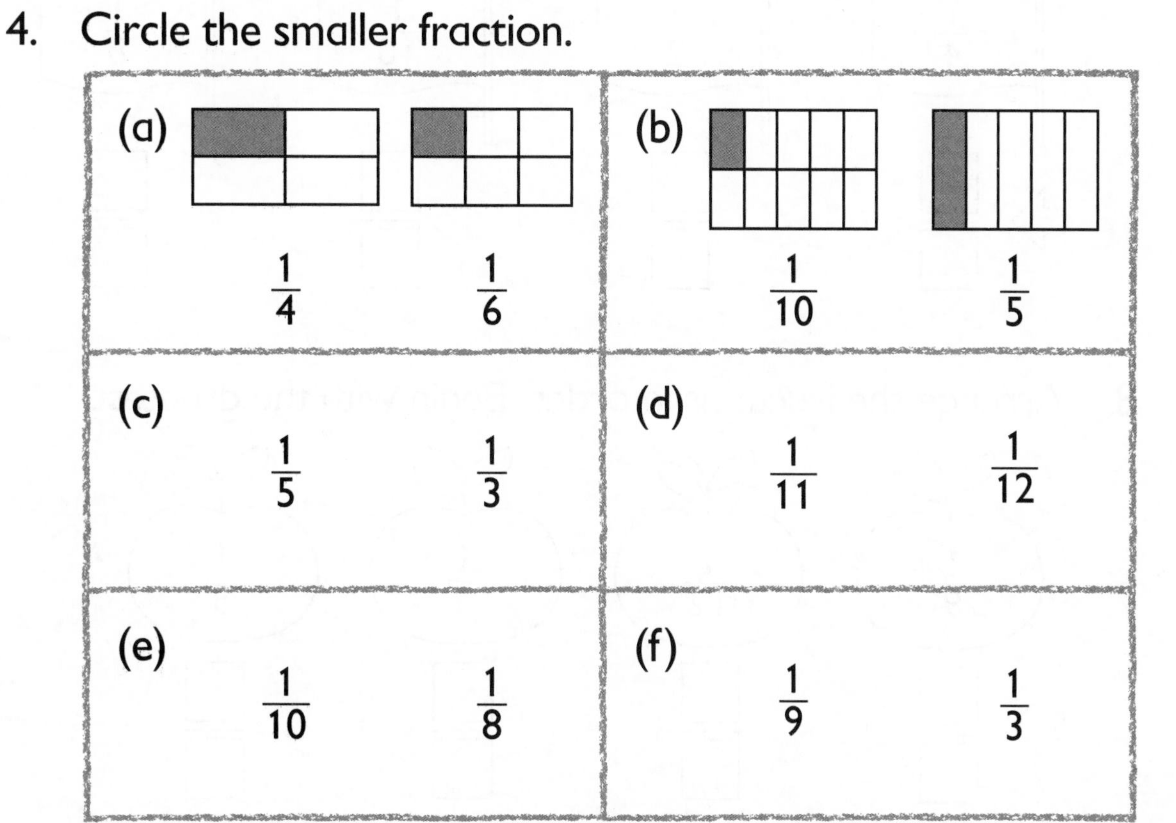

(a) $\frac{1}{4}$ $\frac{1}{6}$

(b) $\frac{1}{10}$ $\frac{1}{5}$

(c) $\frac{1}{5}$ $\frac{1}{3}$

(d) $\frac{1}{11}$ $\frac{1}{12}$

(e) $\frac{1}{10}$ $\frac{1}{8}$

(f) $\frac{1}{9}$ $\frac{1}{3}$

5. Circle the greatest fraction.

(a) $\frac{1}{3}$, $\frac{1}{2}$, $\frac{1}{4}$

(b) $\frac{1}{7}$, $\frac{1}{8}$, $\frac{1}{5}$

(c) $\frac{1}{8}$, $\frac{1}{6}$, $\frac{1}{4}$

(d) $\frac{1}{11}$, $\frac{1}{5}$, $\frac{1}{6}$

6. Circle the smallest fraction.

(a) $\frac{1}{5}$, $\frac{1}{7}$, $\frac{1}{2}$

(b) $\frac{1}{10}$, $\frac{1}{12}$, $\frac{1}{8}$

(c) $\frac{1}{4}$, $\frac{1}{3}$, $\frac{1}{2}$

(d) $\frac{1}{9}$, $\frac{1}{6}$, $\frac{1}{3}$

7. Arrange the fractions in order. Begin with the smallest.

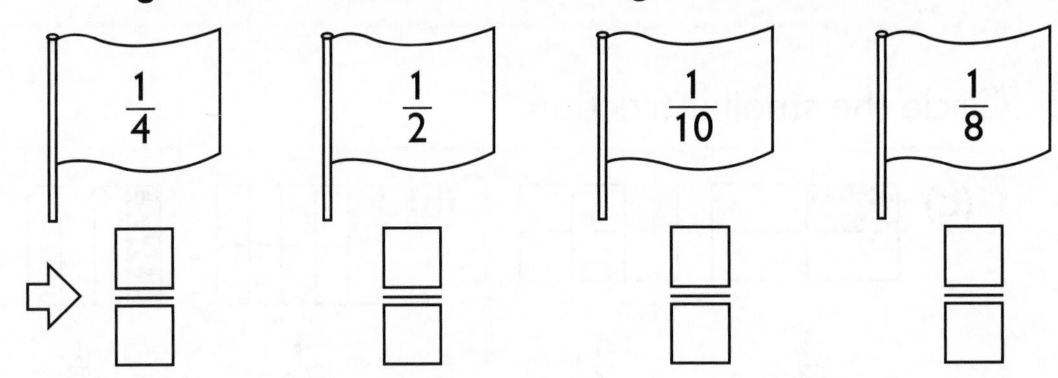

8. Arrange the fractions in order. Begin with the greatest.

EXERCISE 5

1. Write the correct fraction.

(a)

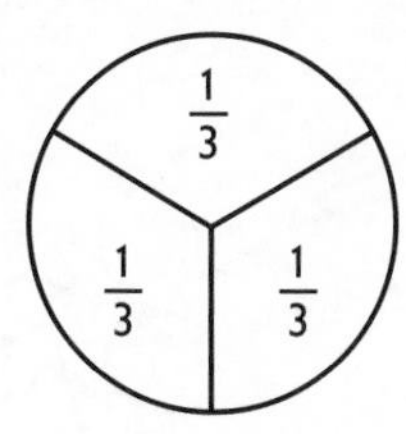

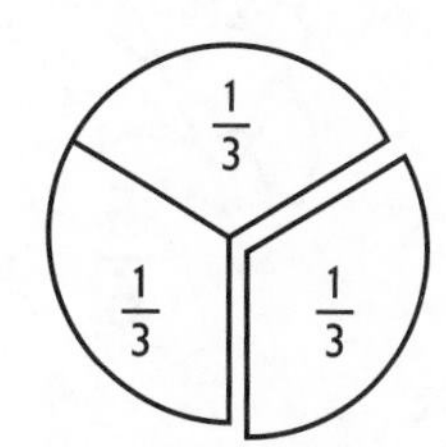

$\frac{1}{3}$ and $\frac{\square}{\square}$ make 1 whole.

(b)

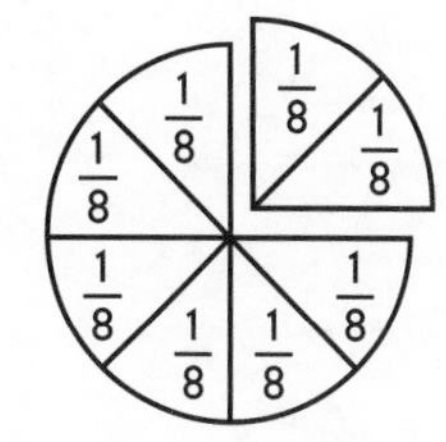

$\frac{2}{8}$ and $\frac{\square}{\square}$ make 1 whole.

(c)

$\frac{2}{5}$ and $\frac{\square}{\square}$ make 1 whole.

(d)

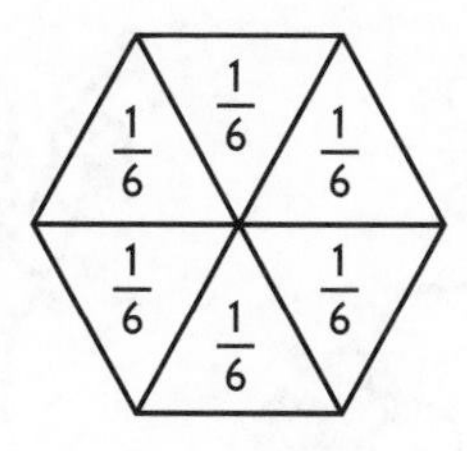

$\frac{1}{6}$ and $\frac{\square}{\square}$ make 1 whole.

2. Join each pair of fractions that add up to 1.

3. (a) Show the fraction $\frac{1}{4}$ on the given number line.

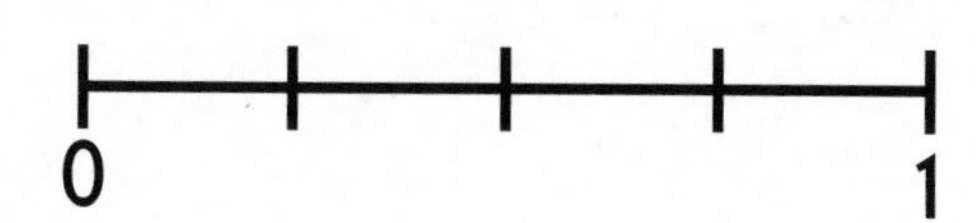

(b) Show the fraction $\frac{2}{3}$ on the given number line.

(c) Show the fraction $\frac{1}{2}$ on the given number line.

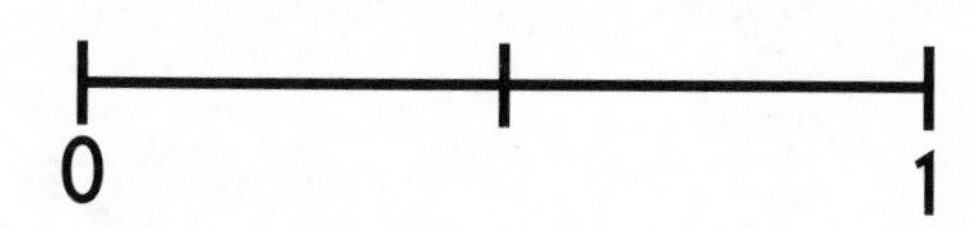

4. Fill in the required fractions on the given number line.

(a) $\frac{1}{4}, \frac{2}{4}, \frac{3}{4}$

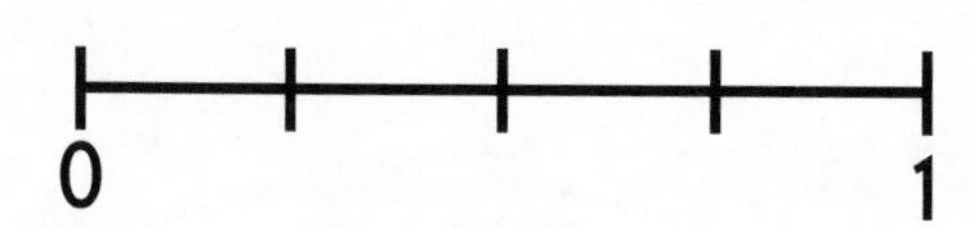

(b) $\frac{1}{3}, \frac{2}{3}$

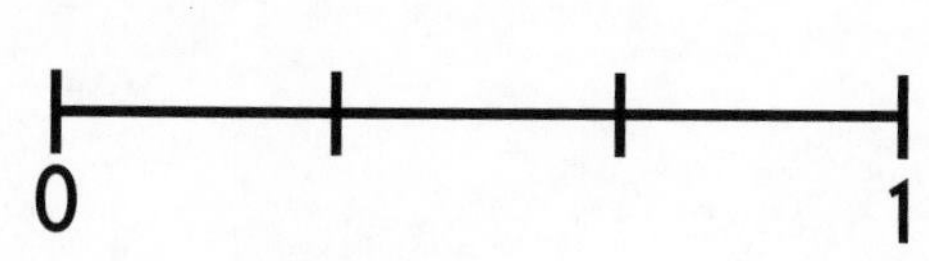

REVIEW 9

1. (a) Color half of the circle.

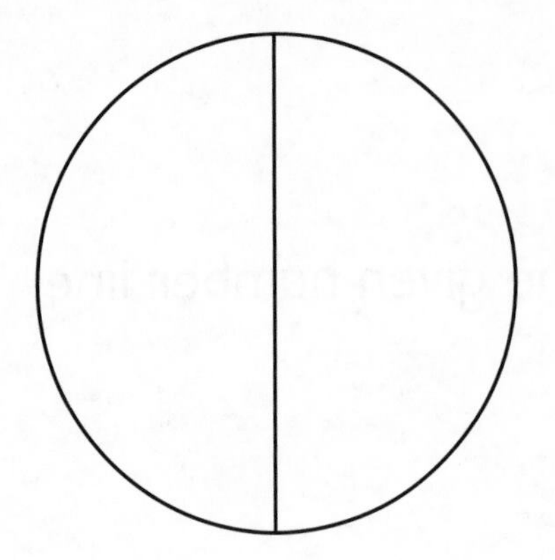

(b) There are ________ halves in a whole.

(c) Color a quarter of the circle.

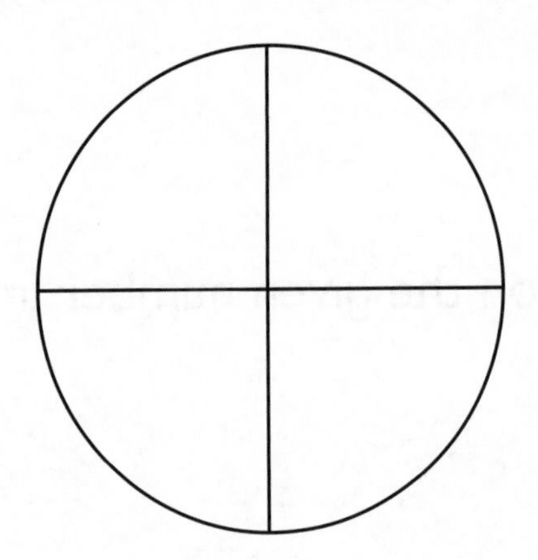

(d) There are ________ fourths in a whole.

2. Fill in the blanks.

(a)

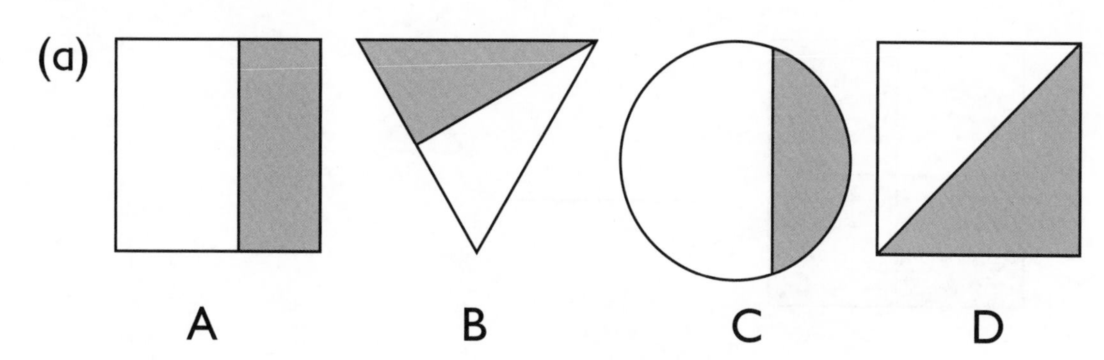

Figures ________ and ________ show $\frac{1}{2}$.

(b)

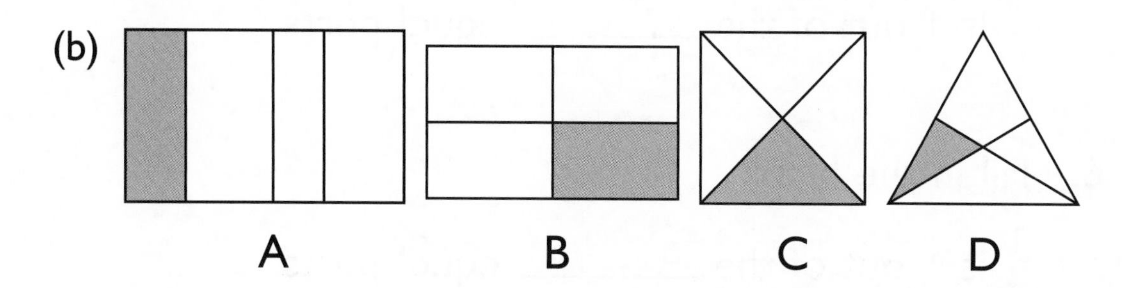

Figures ________ and ________ show $\frac{1}{4}$.

3. (a) Color to show $\frac{1}{2}$.

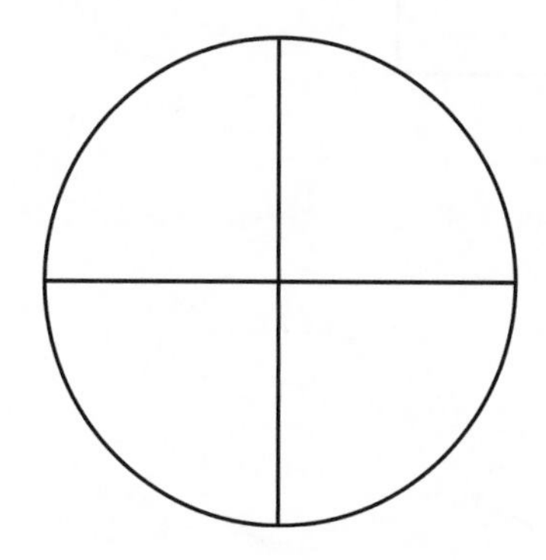

(b) Look at the circle in question 3(a).

Circle the correct answer below.

$\frac{1}{2}$ is (greater than / smaller than) $\frac{1}{4}$.

4. What fraction of the shape is **not** shaded?

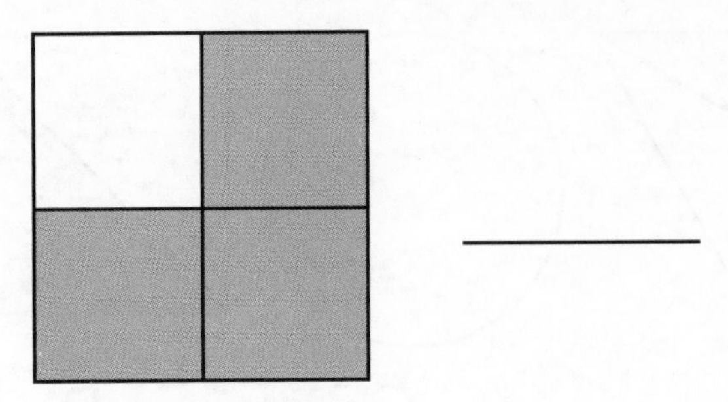

5. Fill in the blank.

$\frac{1}{2}$ is 1 out of the ________ equal parts.

6. Fill in the blank.

$\frac{1}{4}$ is 1 out of the ________ equal parts.

7. Color $\frac{1}{3}$ of the rectangle.

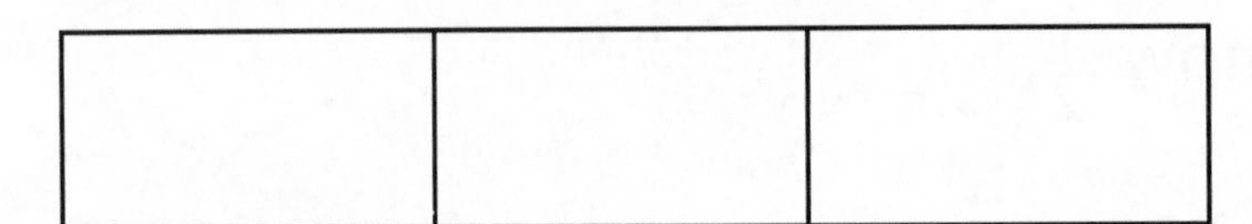

8. Color $\frac{3}{5}$ of the circle.

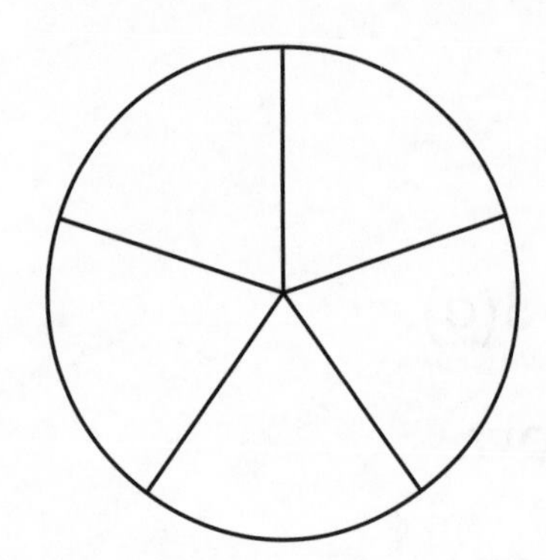

9. Fill in the blanks.

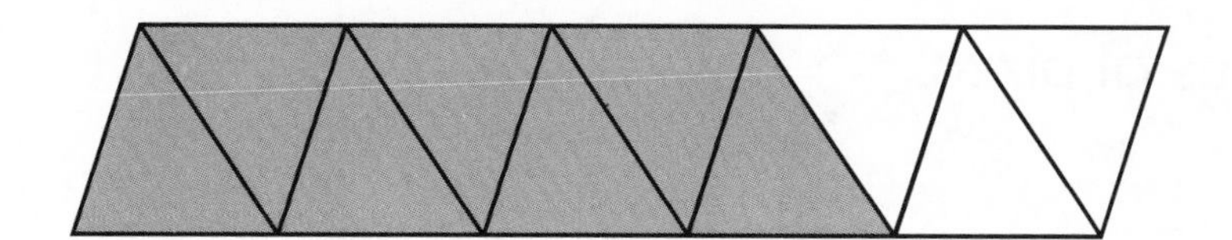

(a) ________ out of the ________ equal parts are shaded.

(b) $\frac{\square}{\square}$ of the shape is shaded.

(c) ________ out of the ________ equal parts are **not** shaded.

(d) $\frac{\square}{\square}$ of the shape is **not** shaded.

10. Which shape shows $\frac{7}{12}$ shaded?

Check ✓ the correct answer.

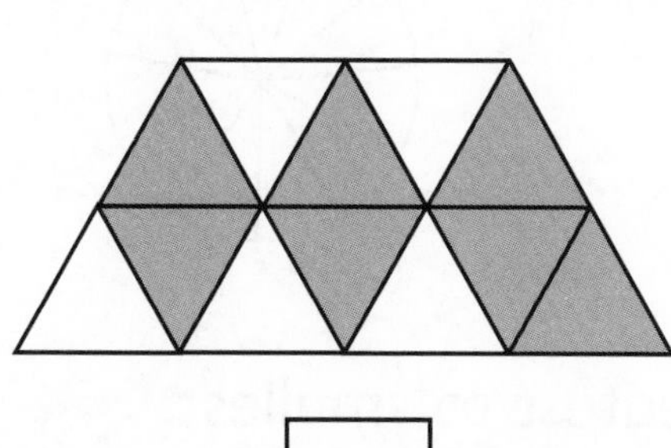

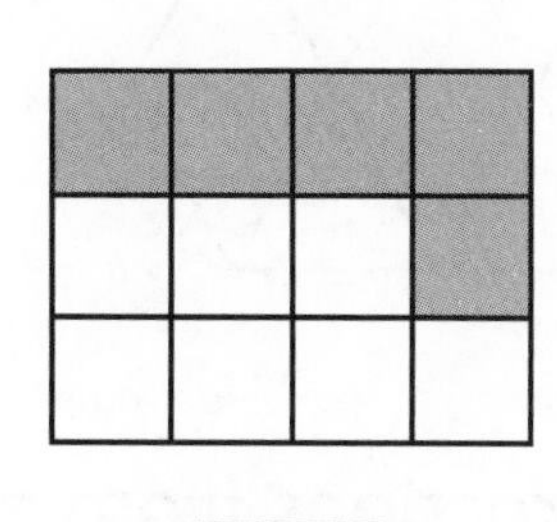

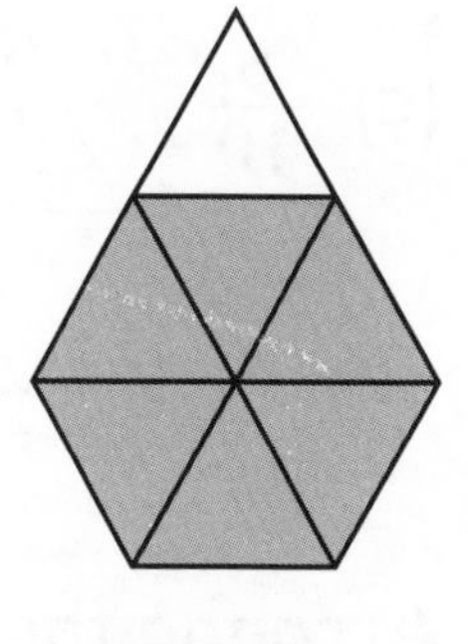

☐ ☐ ☐

11. Fill in the blanks.

Sam ate 5 slices of pizza.

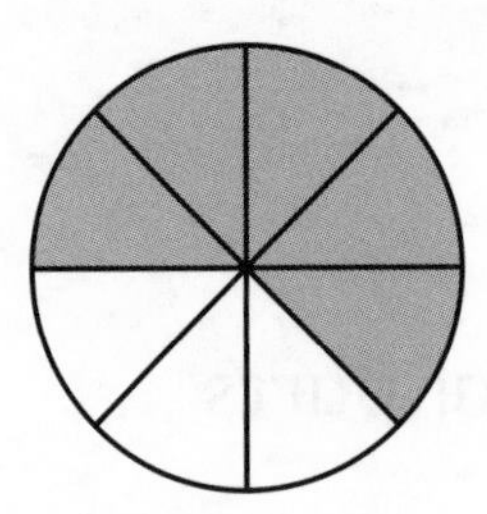

He ate ________ of the pizza.

________ of the pizza was left.

12. Color each picture to show the given fraction.

(a) $\frac{3}{5}$

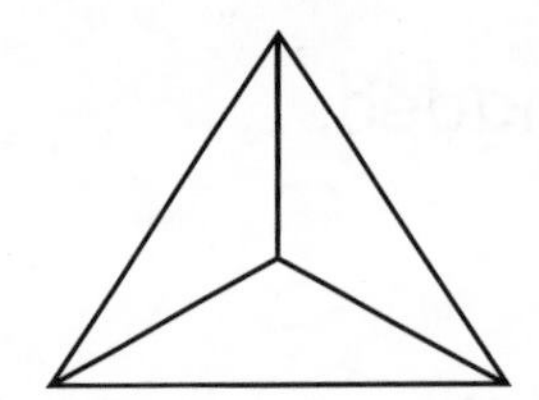

(b) $\frac{4}{8}$

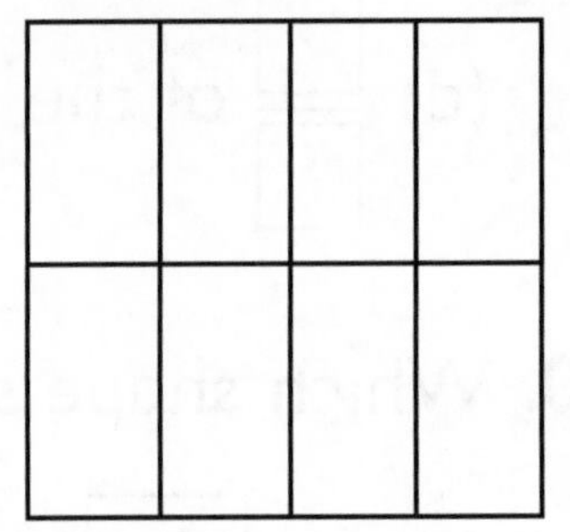

(c) $\frac{6}{10}$

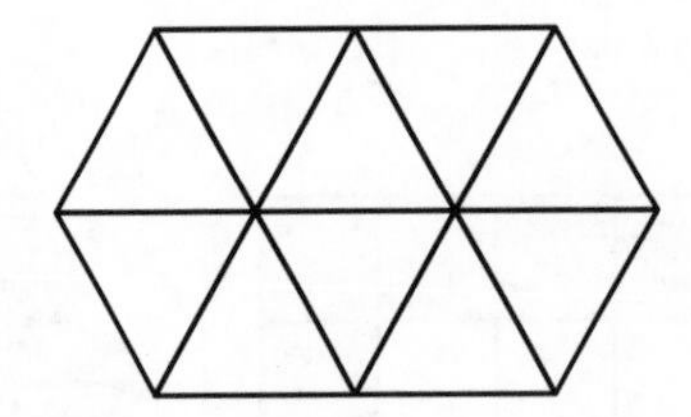

(d) $\frac{5}{11}$

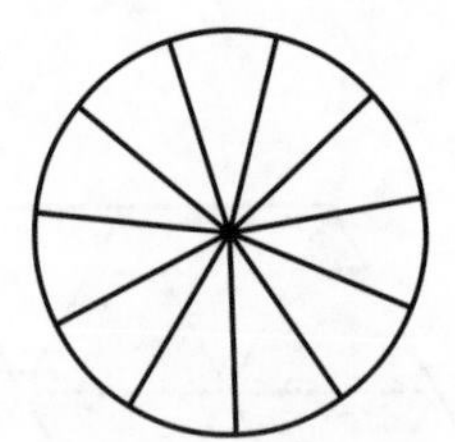

13. Arrange the fractions from greatest to smallest.

$\frac{1}{7}, \frac{1}{2}, \frac{1}{4}$

14. Ms. Smith made 2 cakes that were exactly the same size.
She cut Cake A into fourths and Cake B into sixths.

(a) Which cake had more slices?

(b) Which cake had larger slices?

15. Color to show each pair of fractions.
Then write **>**, **<**, or **=**.

(a)

$\frac{1}{5}$ ◯ $\frac{1}{2}$

(b)

$\frac{1}{3}$ ◯ $\frac{1}{4}$

16. Show the fraction $\frac{3}{4}$ on the given number line.

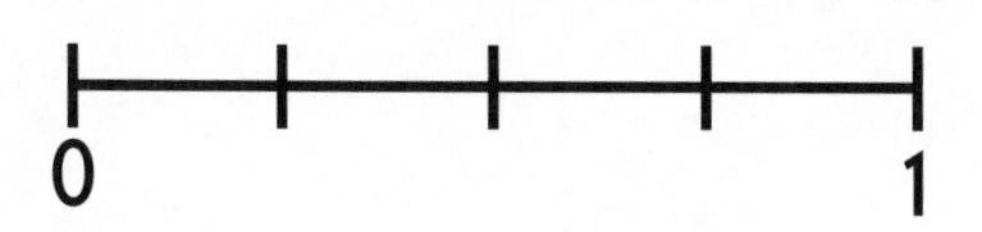

EXERCISE 1

1. Count in steps of 5 minutes.
   Write the missing numbers.

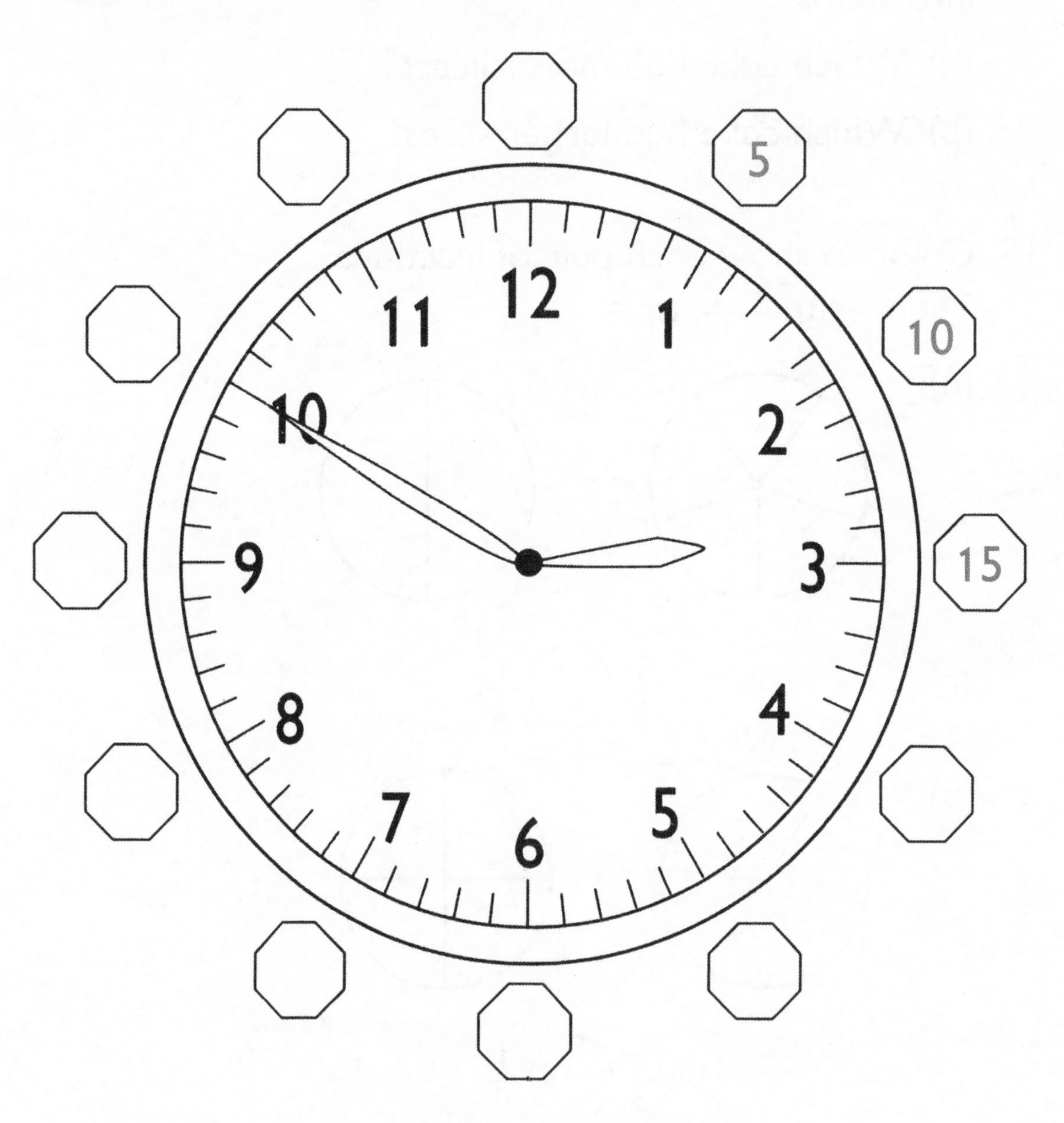

The time is ________ minutes after 2 o'clock.

2. Write the time shown on each clock face.

(a)

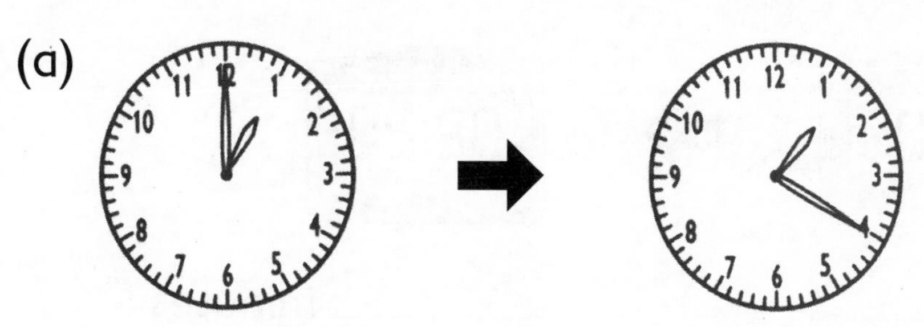

1 o'clock

20 minutes after 1 o'clock

1:00

1:20

(b)

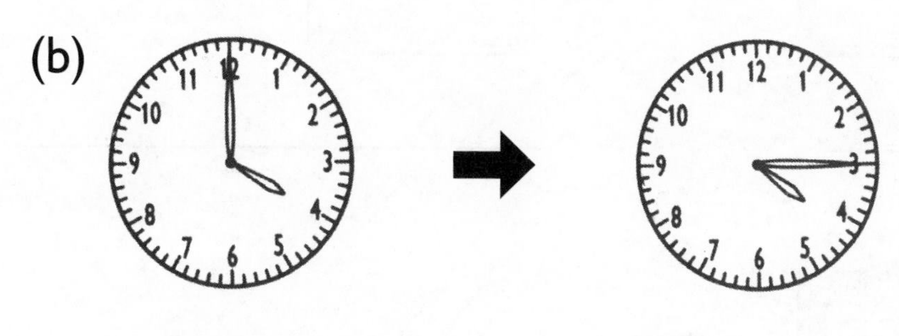

4 o'clock

_____ minutes after 4 o'clock

_____

_____

(c)

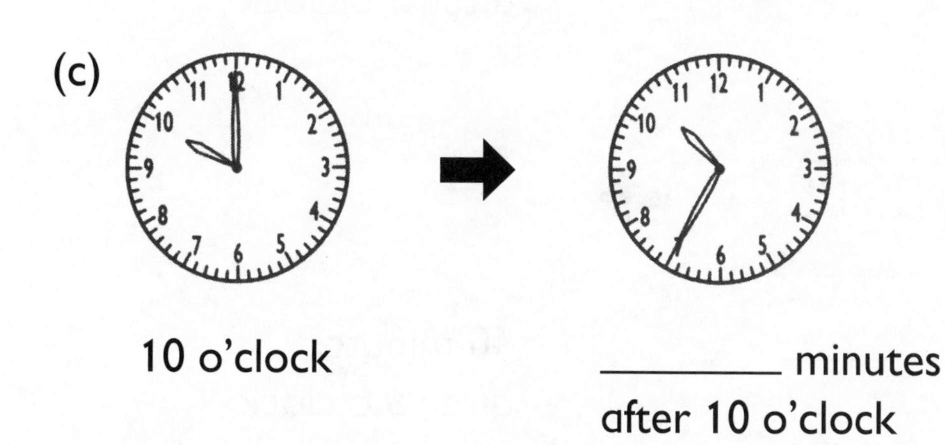

10 o'clock

_____ minutes after 10 o'clock

_____

_____

3. Write the time shown on each clock.

(a)

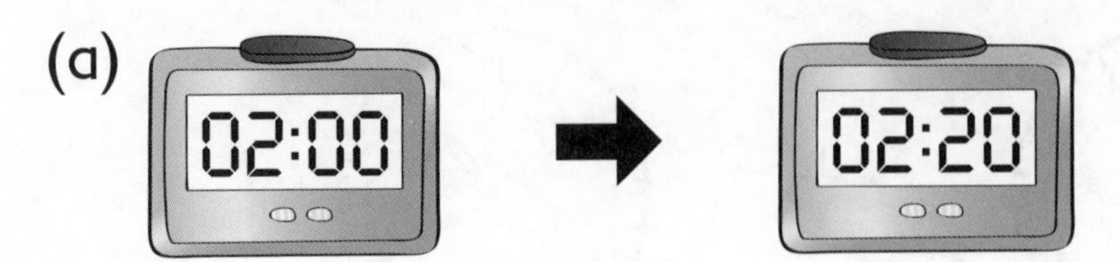

________   ________ minutes after 2 o'clock

(b)

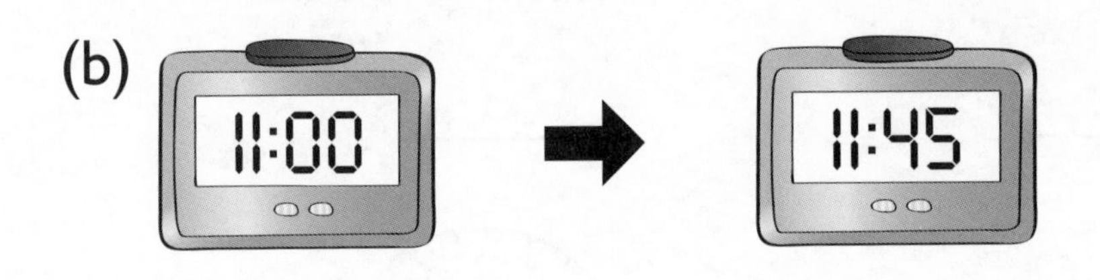

________   ____________________

(c)

________   30 minutes after 5 o'clock

(d)

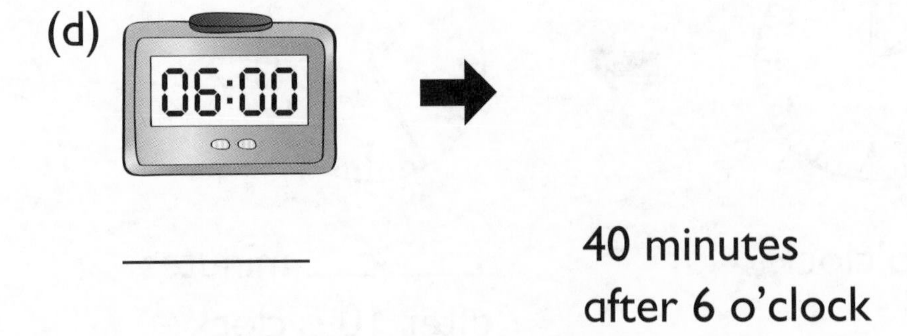

________   40 minutes after 6 o'clock

4. What time is shown on each clock face?
Match the clocks to the correct answers.

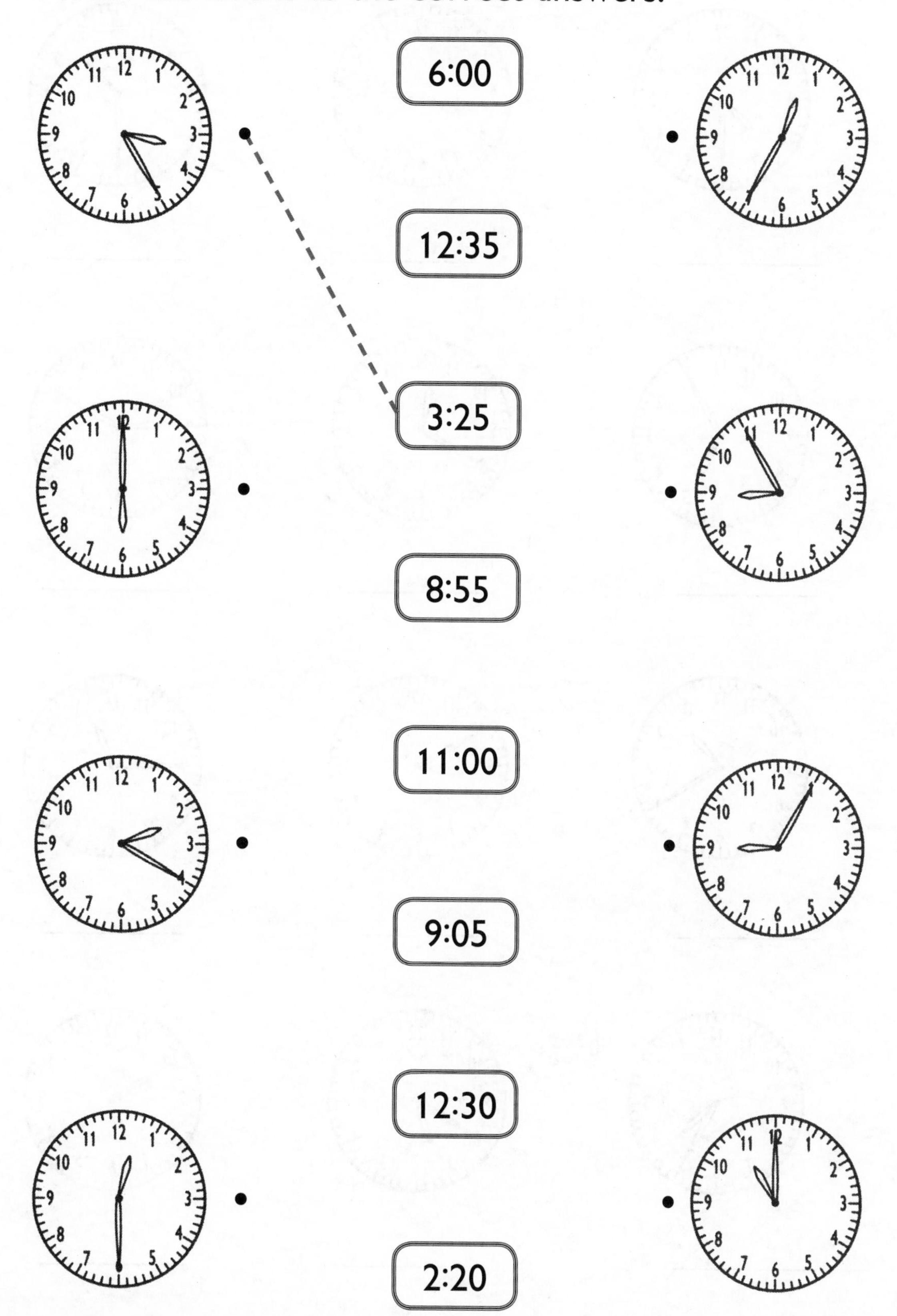

5. What time is it?

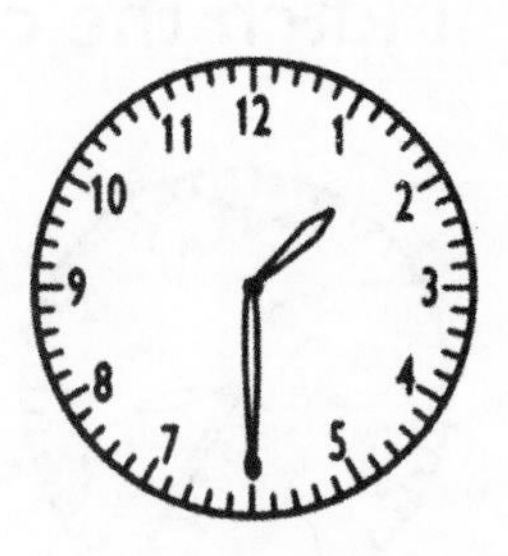

7:30

EXERCISE 2

1. Fill in the blanks.

(a)

________ minutes after ________ o'clock

________ minutes past ________

(b)

________ minutes after ________ o'clock

________ minutes past ________

(c)

________ minutes before ________ o'clock

________ minutes to ________

(d)

________ minutes before ________ o'clock

________ minutes to ________

2. Fill in the blanks.

(a)

6:10

_________ minutes past _________

(b)

6:45

_________ minutes to _________

(c)

7:15

_________ minutes past _________

(d)

7:35

_________ minutes to _________

3. Draw the minute hand on each clock face to show the time. Write A.M. or P.M.

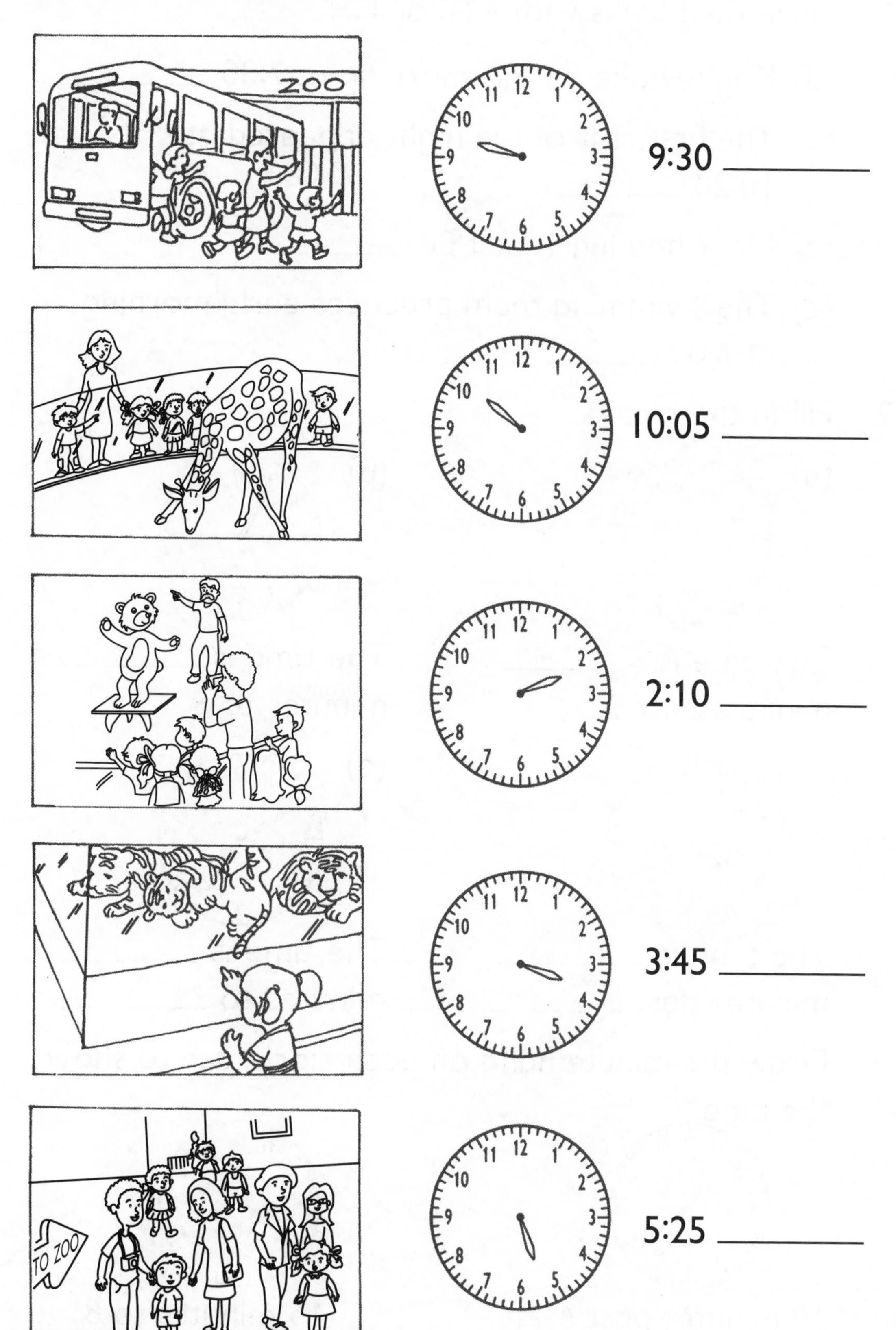

REVIEW 10

1. Fill in the blanks with A.M. or P.M.

   (a) Kayla woke up this morning at 7:00 ________

   (b) The first star of the night appeared at 10:20 ________

   (c) Mark had lunch at 1:00 ________

   (d) The swimming team practices early morning at 6:00 ________

2. Fill in the blanks.

(a)

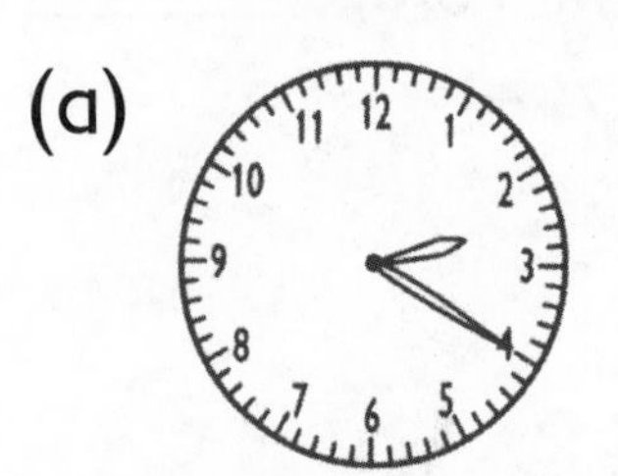

The time is ________ minutes past 2.

(b)

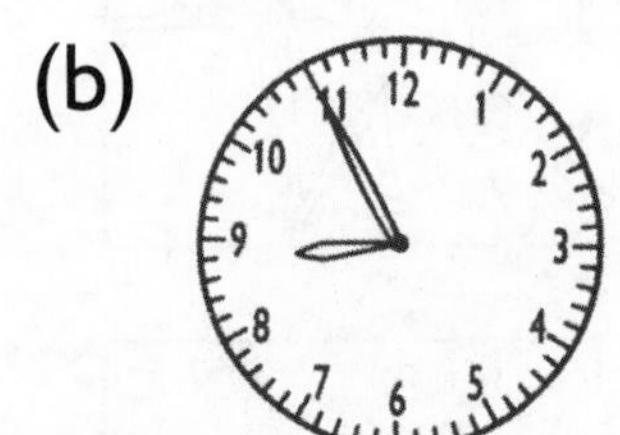

The time is ________ minutes to 9.

(c)

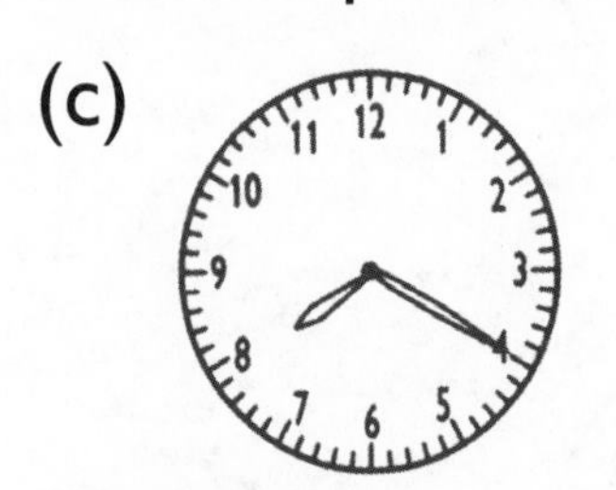

The time is ________ minutes past ________

(d)

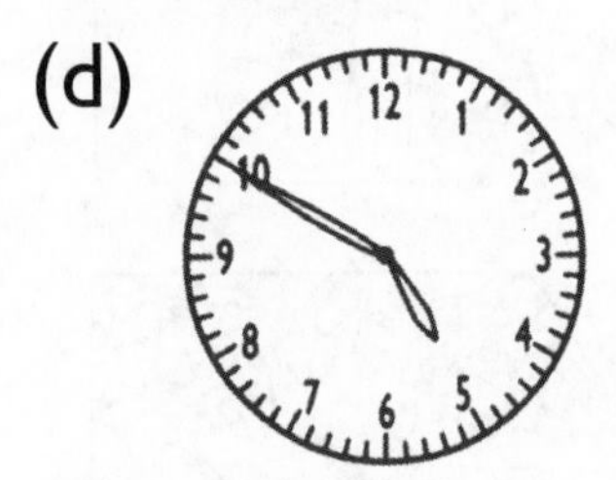

The time is ________ minutes to ________.

3. Draw the minute hand on each clock face to show the time.

10 minutes past 4

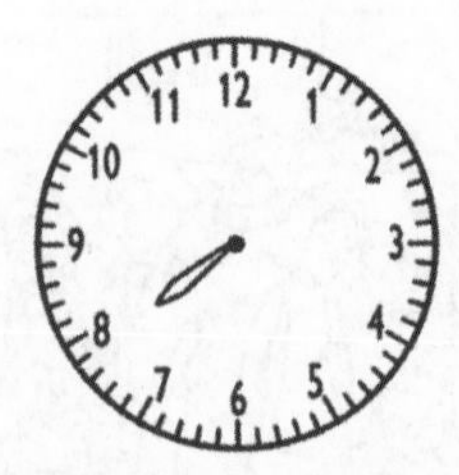

15 minutes to 8

EXERCISE 1

1. A group of children made this tally chart to show the colors they like best.

Color	
Red	卌 III
Green	IIII
Yellow	III
Blue	卌 I

Study the tally chart.
Then fill in the blanks.

(a) ________ children like yellow best.

(b) ________ children like blue best.

(c) ________ more children like blue better than green.

(d) ________ is the most popular color.

(e) ________ is the least popular color.

2. This picture graph shows the amounts of money four boys have.

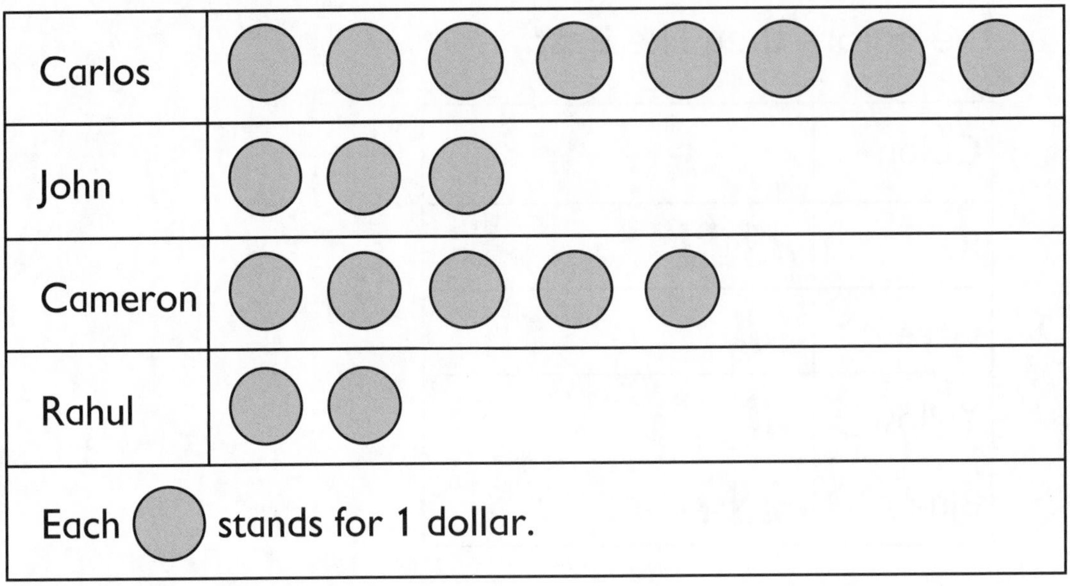

Carlos	● ● ● ● ● ● ● ●
John	● ● ●
Cameron	● ● ● ● ●
Rahul	● ●
Each ● stands for 1 dollar.	

Study the graph.
Then fill in the blanks.

(a) Carlos has ________ dollars.

(b) Cameron has ________ dollars.

(c) Carlos has ________ dollars more than John.

(d) Rahul has ________ dollars less than Cameron.

(e) ________ has 3 dollars less than Carlos.

3. Joe made this picture graph to show the number of different types of toys he has.

Action figures	Robots	Cars	Airplanes
▲▲▲▲▲	▲▲▲▲	▲▲▲▲▲▲▲	▲▲

Each ▲ stands for 2 toys.

Study the graph.
Then fill in the blanks.

(a) Joe has ________ action figures.

(b) He has ________ cars.

(c) He has ________ airplanes.

(d) He has ________ more cars than robots.

(e) He has ________ fewer airplanes than action figures.

4.

Dionne

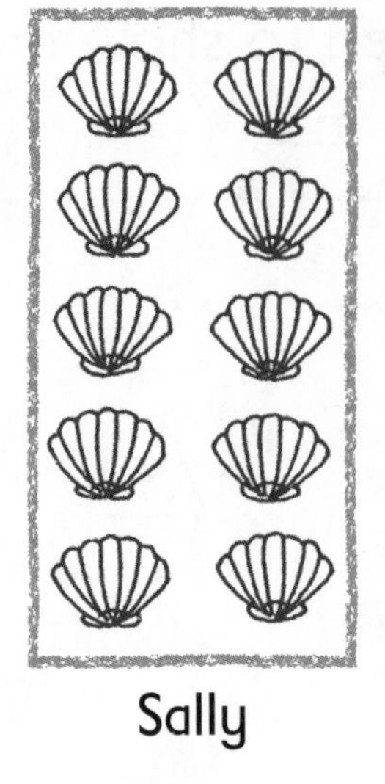

Sally

Ling

Amit

Count the shells collected by each girl.
Then complete the following picture graph.

Dionne	Sally	Ling	Amit
Each ◯ stands for 2 shells.			

EXERCISE 2

1. Fill in the blanks.

   (a) Each ☆ stands for 5 fish.

   ☆☆ stand for ________ fish.

   (b) Each ◇ stands for 10 cars.

   ◇◇◇ stand for ________ cars.

   (c) Each ○ stands for 4 people.

   ○○○ stand for ________ people.

2. (a) Each □ stands for 3 balloons.
   Color the correct number of squares to show 15 balloons.

   □ □ □ □ □ □ □ □ □ □

   (b) Each △ stands for 10 flowers.
   Color the correct number of triangles to show 60 flowers.

   △ △ △ △ △ △ △ △ △ △

3. This picture graph shows David's savings in four months.

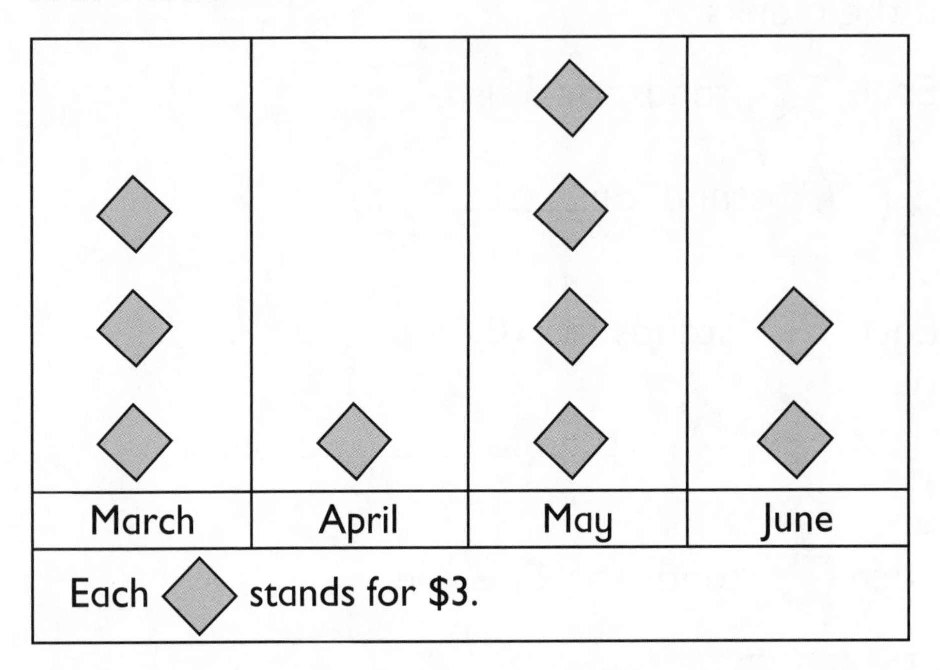

Study the graph. Complete the table below.

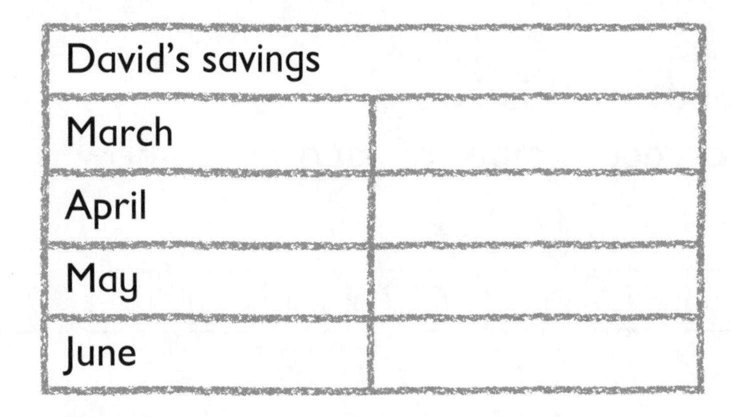

David's savings	
March	
April	
May	
June	

Then fill in the blanks.

(a) He saved $________ more in May than in April.

(b) His total savings in the 4 months was $________.

(c) He saved $6 less in April than in ________.

4. This picture graph shows the number of stamps collected by four children.

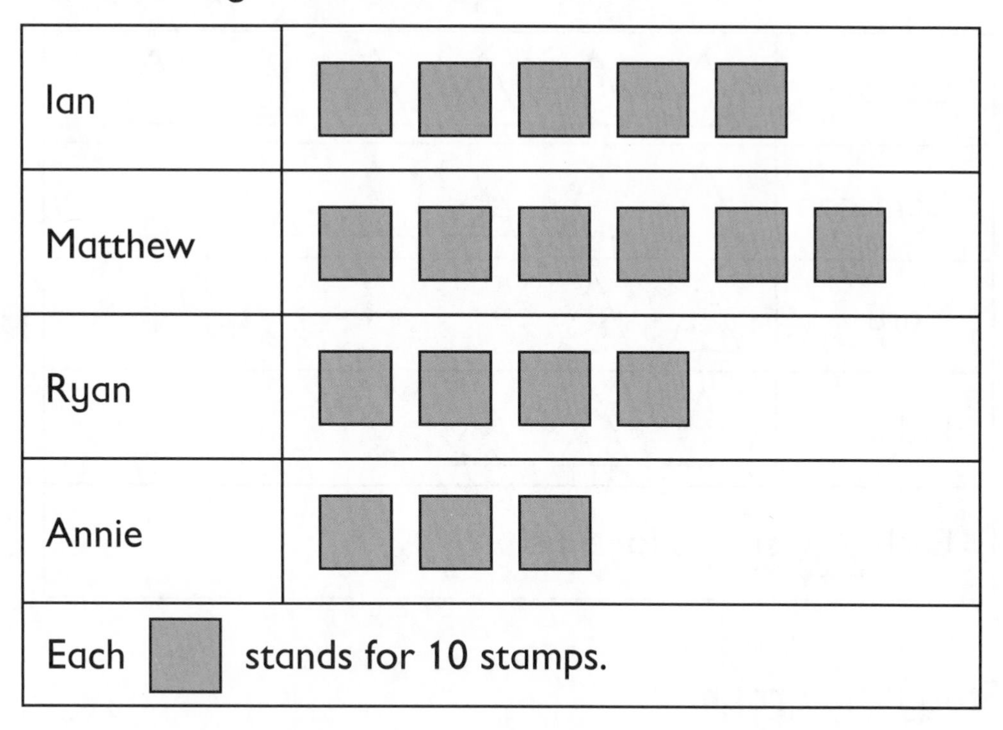

Study the graph. Then fill in the blanks.

(a) Ian collected ________ stamps.

(b) ________ collected the greatest number of stamps.

(c) ________ collected 30 stamps.

(d) Ian collected ________ more stamps than Ryan.

(e) Annie collected ________ fewer stamps than Matthew.

(f) Ryan and Annie collected ________ stamps altogether.

5. This picture graph shows the number of fish caught by four children.

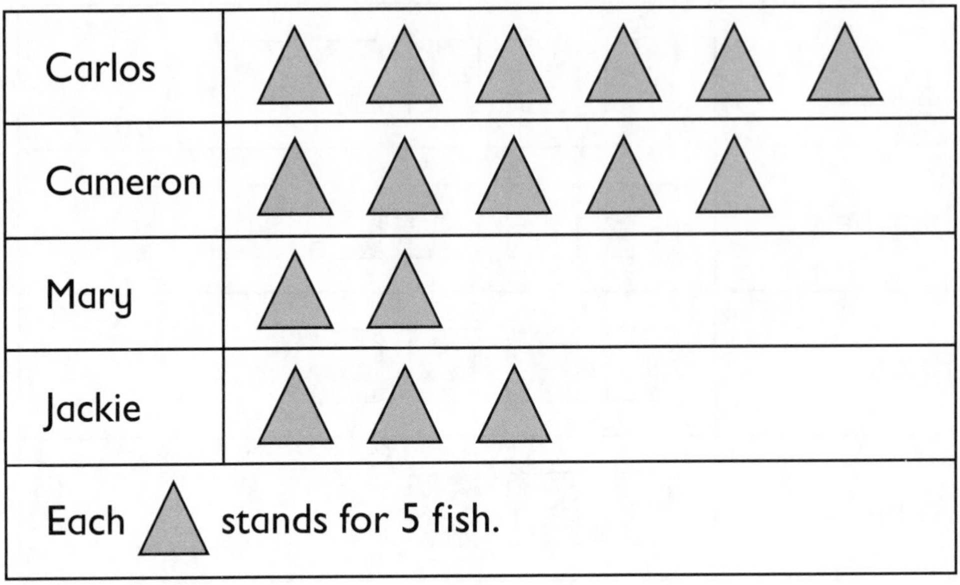

Carlos	▲ ▲ ▲ ▲ ▲ ▲
Cameron	▲ ▲ ▲ ▲ ▲
Mary	▲ ▲
Jackie	▲ ▲ ▲
Each ▲ stands for 5 fish.	

Study the graph.
Write **Yes** or **No** for each of the following:

(a) Carlos caught 6 fish.	
(b) Jackie caught 15 fish.	
(c) Cameron caught 2 more fish than Jackie.	
(d) Mary caught 20 fewer fish than Carlos.	
(e) If Carlos caught 2 more fish, he would have 20 fish.	

EXERCISE 3

1. This table shows the number of birds in each group.

A	5
B	10
C	11
D	8

Use the table to color the graph.

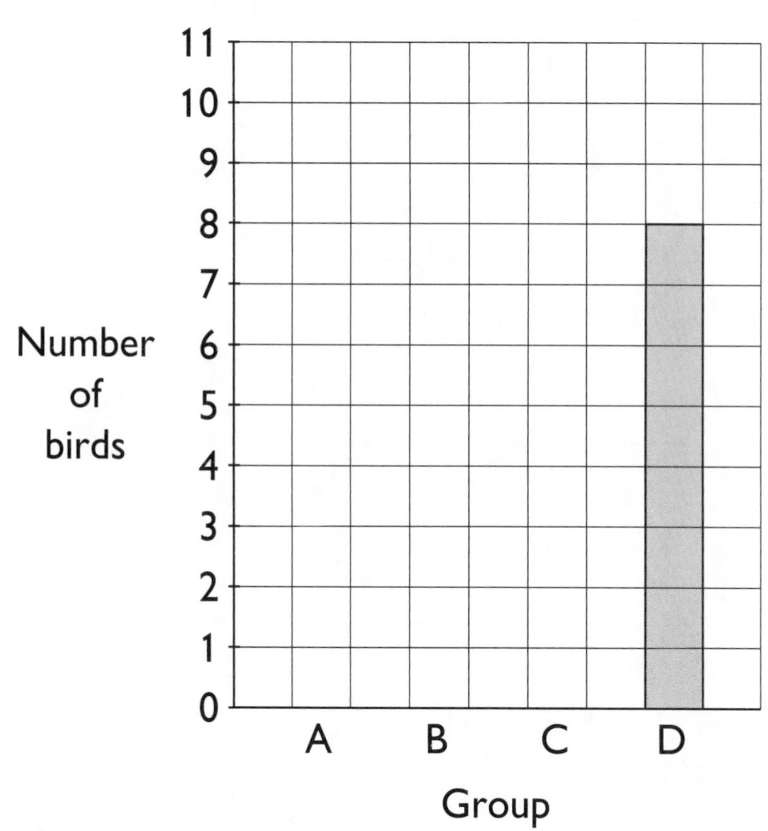

Fill in the blanks.

(a) There are ________ more birds in Group C than in Group A.

(b) There are ________ times as many birds in Group B as in Group A.

(c) There are ________ birds altogether.

2. This table shows the number of students in each group.

A	21
B	16
C	17
D	8

Use the table to color the graph.

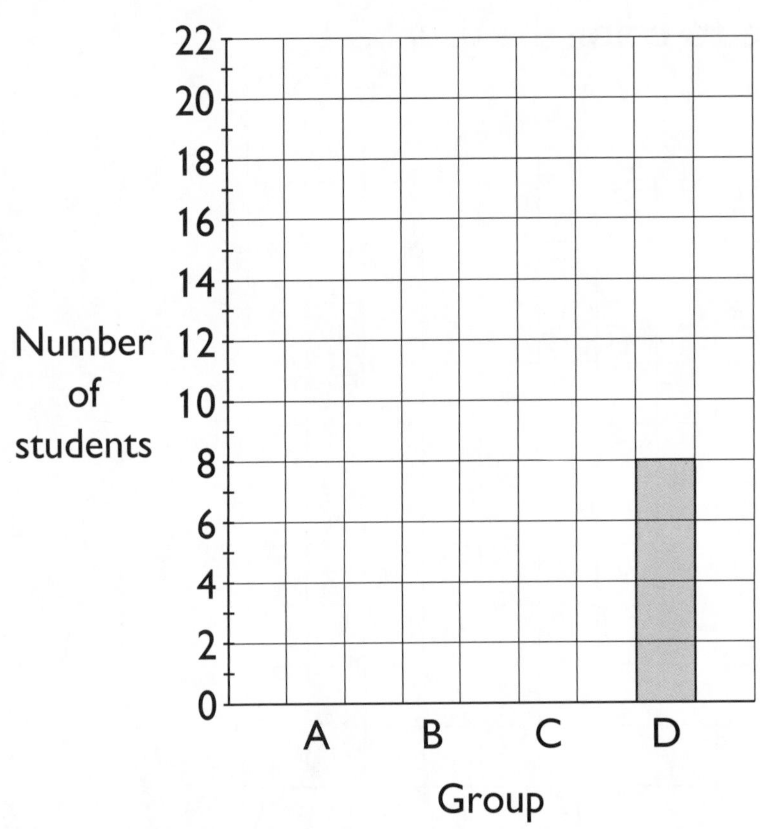

Fill in the blanks.

(a) There are ________ more students in Group A than in Group C.

(b) There are ________ times as many students in Group B as in Group D.

(c) There are ________ students altogether.

3. This bar graph shows the number of books read by five girls.

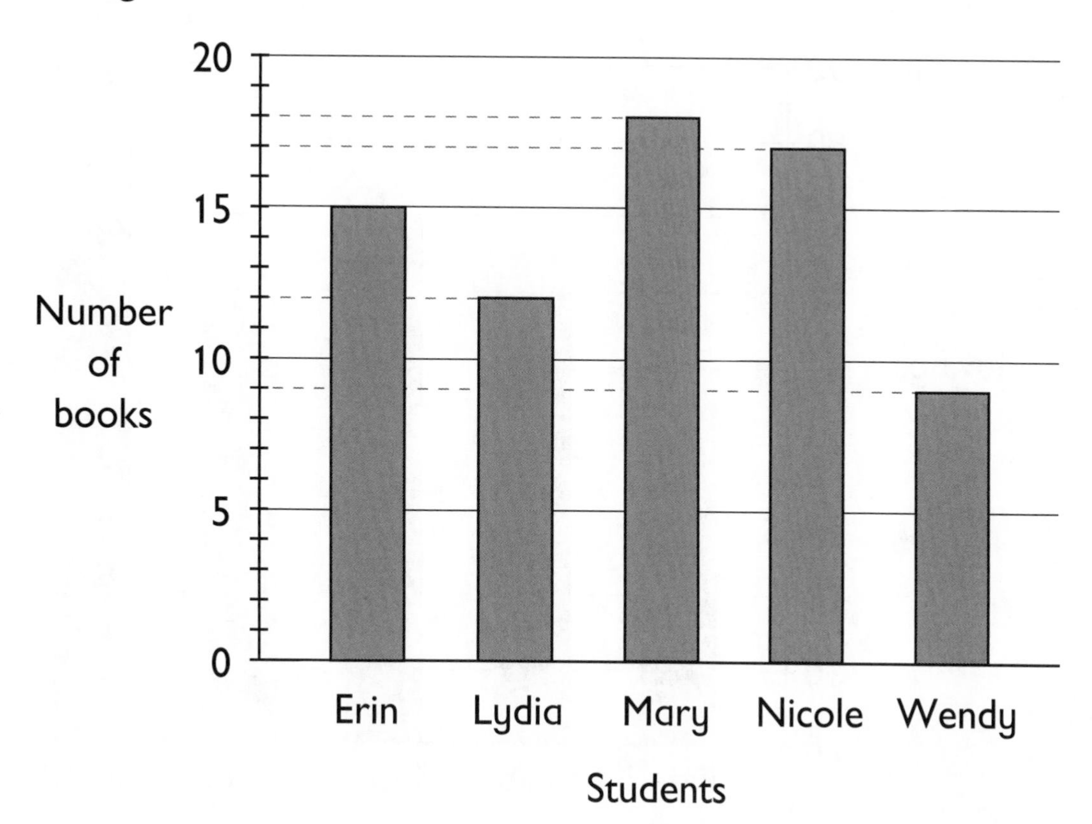

Study the graph and fill in the blanks.

(a) Lydia read ________ books.

(b) ________ read the most books.

She read ________ books.

(c) ________ read the fewest books.

She read ________ books.

(d) Mary read twice as many books as ________.

4. This bar graph shows the savings of five students.

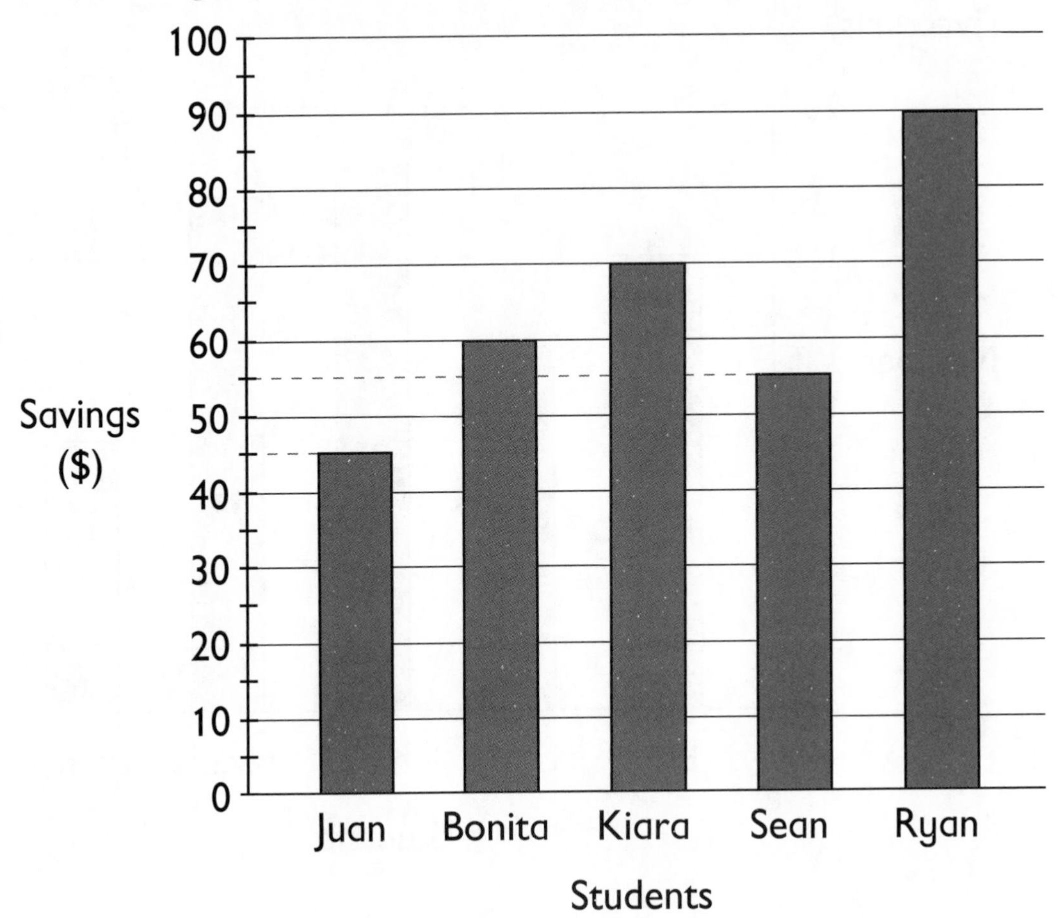

Study the graph and fill in the blanks.

(a) Juan saved $________.

(b) Kiara saved $________ more than Bonita.

(c) ________ saved the most.

(d) The total savings of Bonita, Kiara, and Sean was $________.

5. This table shows the amount of money saved by five boys.

Name	Amount
John	$30
Dylan	$45
Sam	$25
David	$10
Sanjay	$20

(a) Complete the bar graph and fill in the blanks.

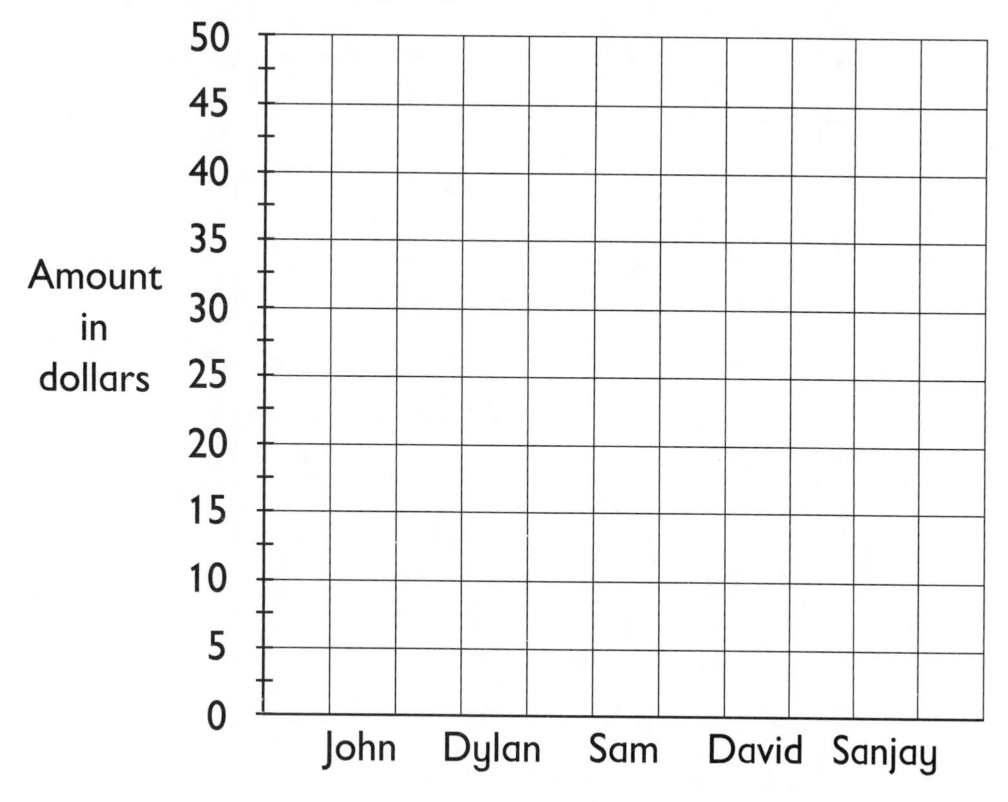

(b) Dylan saved ________ more than David.

(c) Sanjay saved ________ less than John.

EXERCISE 4

1. This table shows the ages of some children who went for a nature hike.

Age in years	6	7	8	9	10	11
Number of children	4	9	12	18	11	3

Complete the following line plot to show the data given in the table.

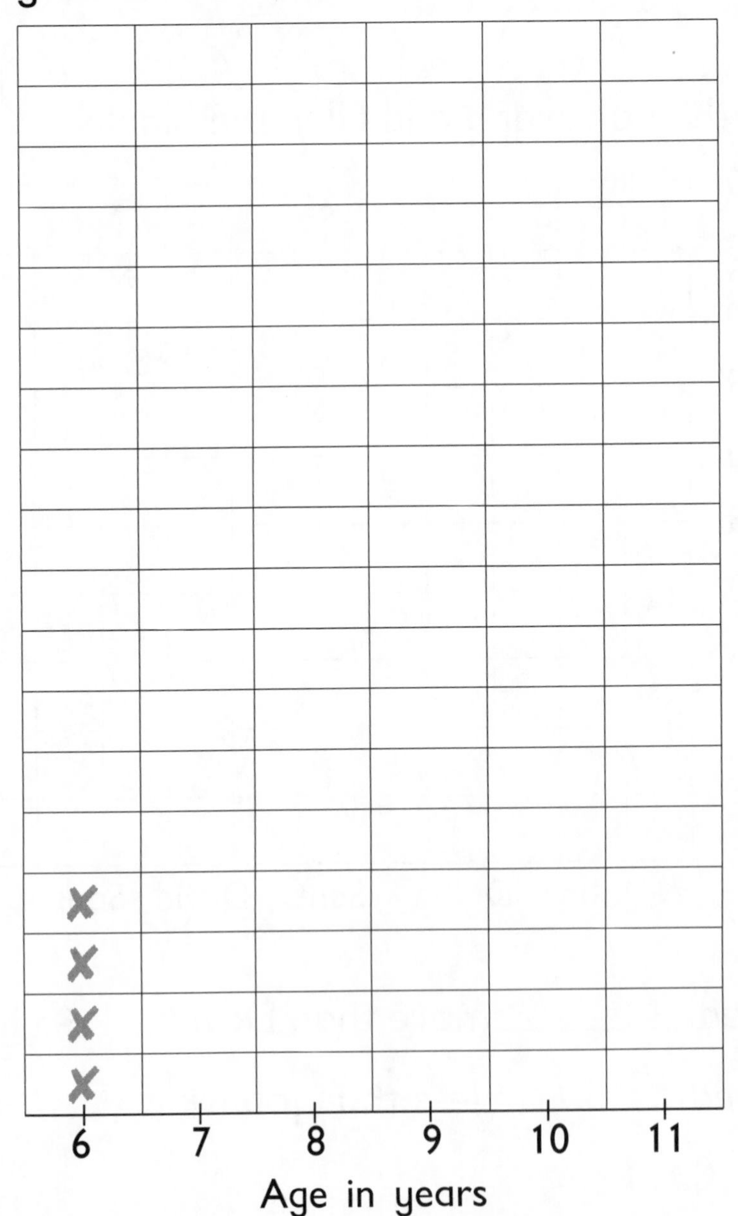

(a) How many children went on the nature hike?

____

(b) What is the most common age of the children who went on the hike? _________

(c) If the nature center were to create a nature show for children, which age group should the show be created for to get the most interest? _________

2. This line plot shows the heights of some growing tomato plants in Mary's garden.

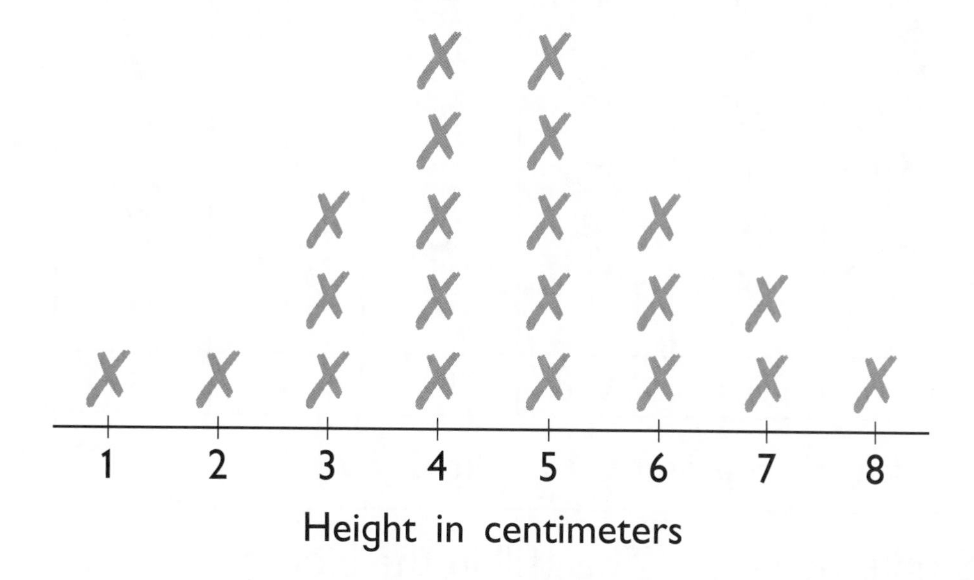

(a) How many plants are there? _________

(b) What are the two most common heights of the growing tomato plants? _________

REVIEW 11

1. The picture graph shows the number of chickens sold at a farm.

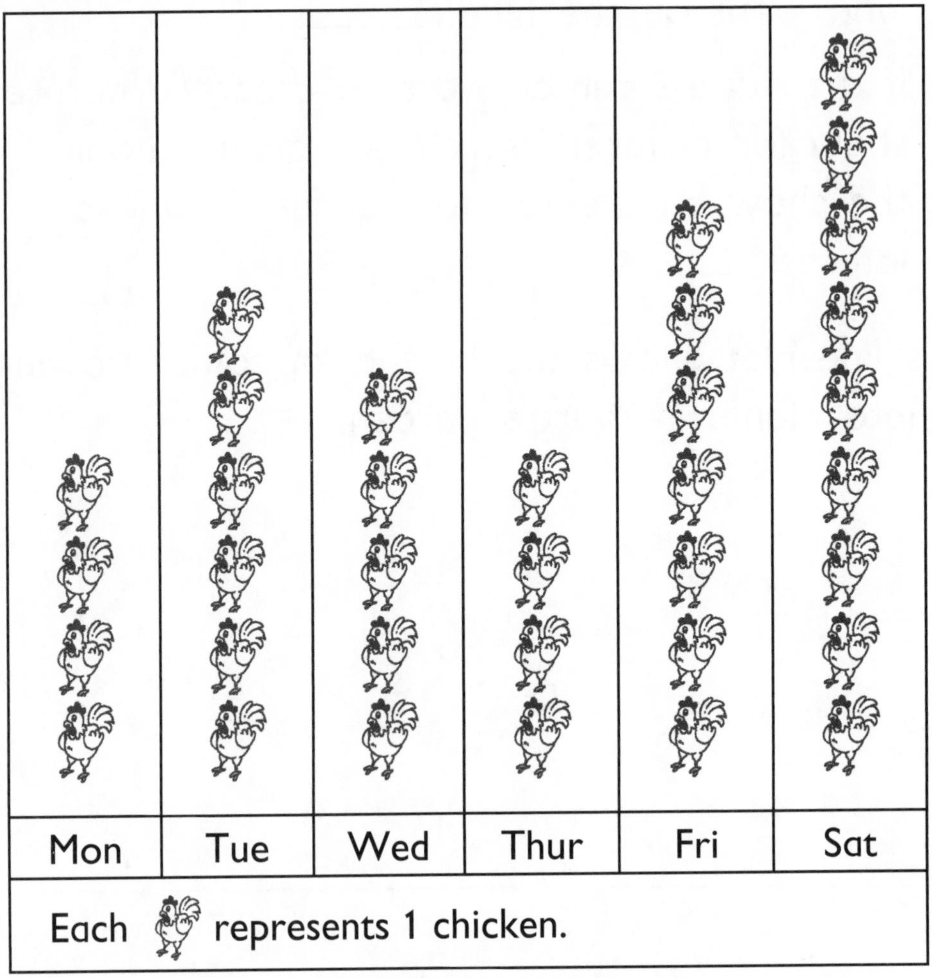

Mon	Tue	Wed	Thur	Fri	Sat

Each represents 1 chicken.

Study the graph. Then fill in the blanks.

(a) ________ chickens were sold on Saturday.

(b) The number of chickens sold on ________ and on ________ is the same.

(c) ________ more chickens were sold on Friday than on Wednesday.

(d) ________ chickens were sold on Tuesday.

(e) The total number of chickens sold from Monday to Saturday is ________.

2. The picture graph below shows the number of books read by four children.

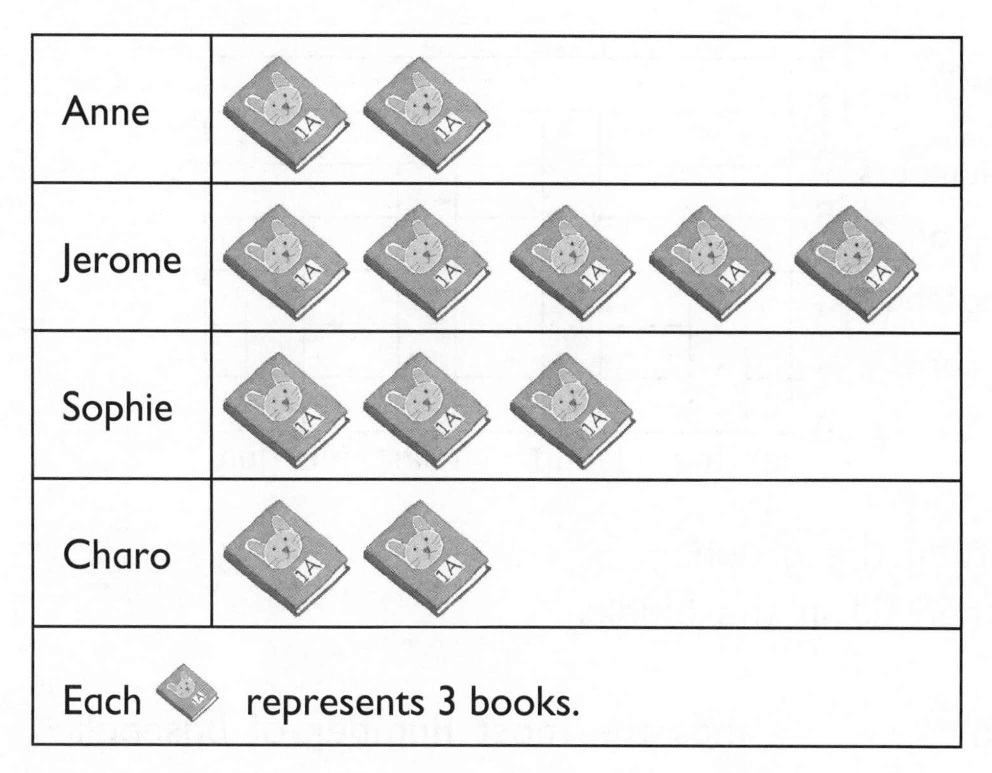

Study the graph. Then fill in the blanks.

(a) ________ read the most number of books.

(b) Sophie read ________ books.

(c) ________ and ________ read the same number of books.

(d) Jerome and Anne read a total of ________ books.

(e) Charo read ________ fewer books than Sophie.

(f) The total number of books read by the 4 children is ________.

3. The bar graph shows the number of baseball cards four children have.

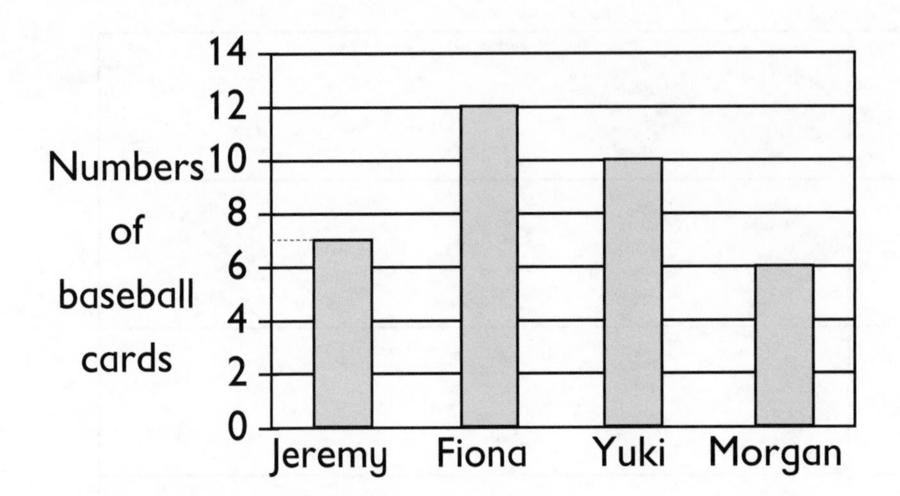

Study the graph.
Then fill in the blanks.

(a) ________ has the most number of baseball cards.

(b) Morgan has ________ baseball cards.

(c) Jeremy and Fiona have ________ baseball cards altogether.

(d) Yuki has ________ more baseball cards than Jeremy.

(e) The 4 children have ________ baseball cards altogether.

4. 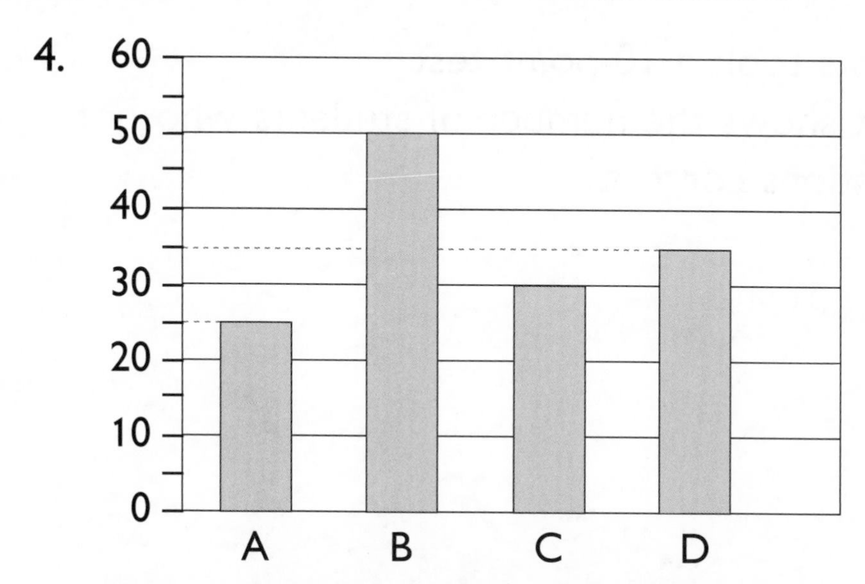

Four groups of students played a game.
Which group scored 5 more points than Group A?

Group ________ scored 5 more points than Group A.

5. This bar graph shows the number of potted plants in four gardens, A, B, C, and D.

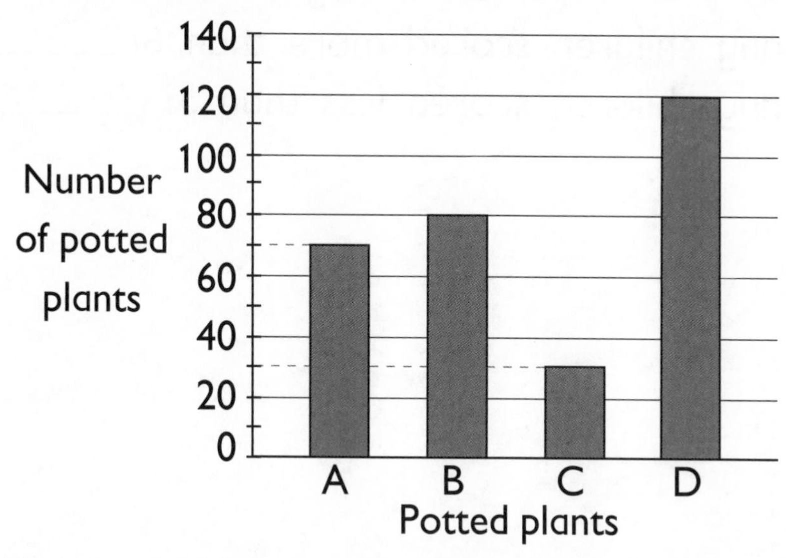

Study the graph and answer these questions.

(a) How many more potted plants are there in Garden D than in Garden A? ________

(b) How many potted plants are there altogether in the four gardens? ________

6. Some students took a 10-point test.
The line plot shows the number of students who got 1 to 10 questions correct.

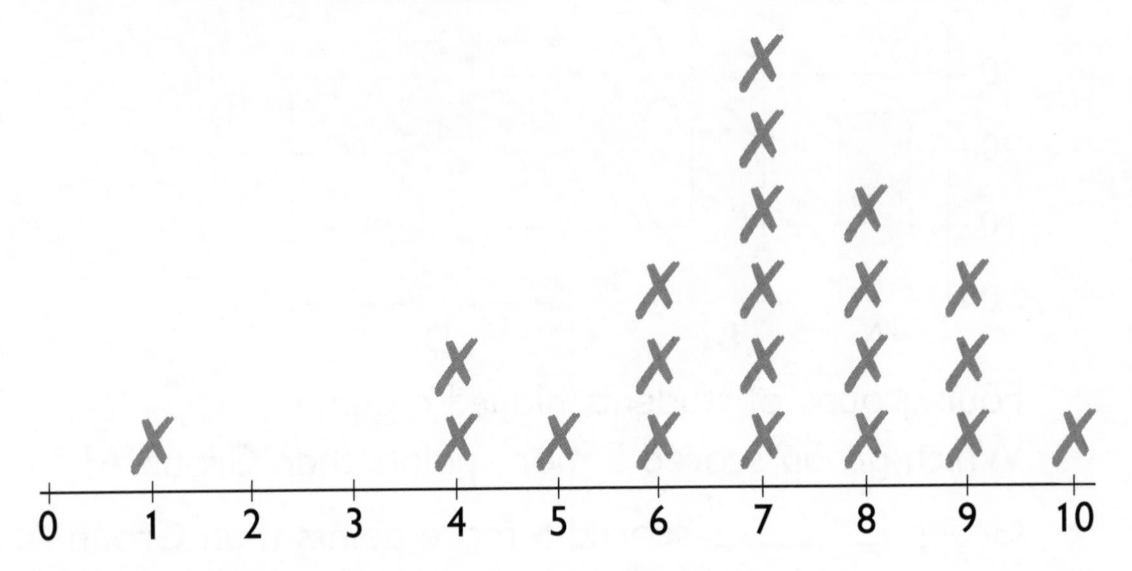

(a) How many children took the test? ________

(b) What score did most children get? ________

(c) How many children scored more than 6? ________

(d) How many children scored less than 5? ________

EXERCISE 1

1. Join each pair of objects that have similar shapes.

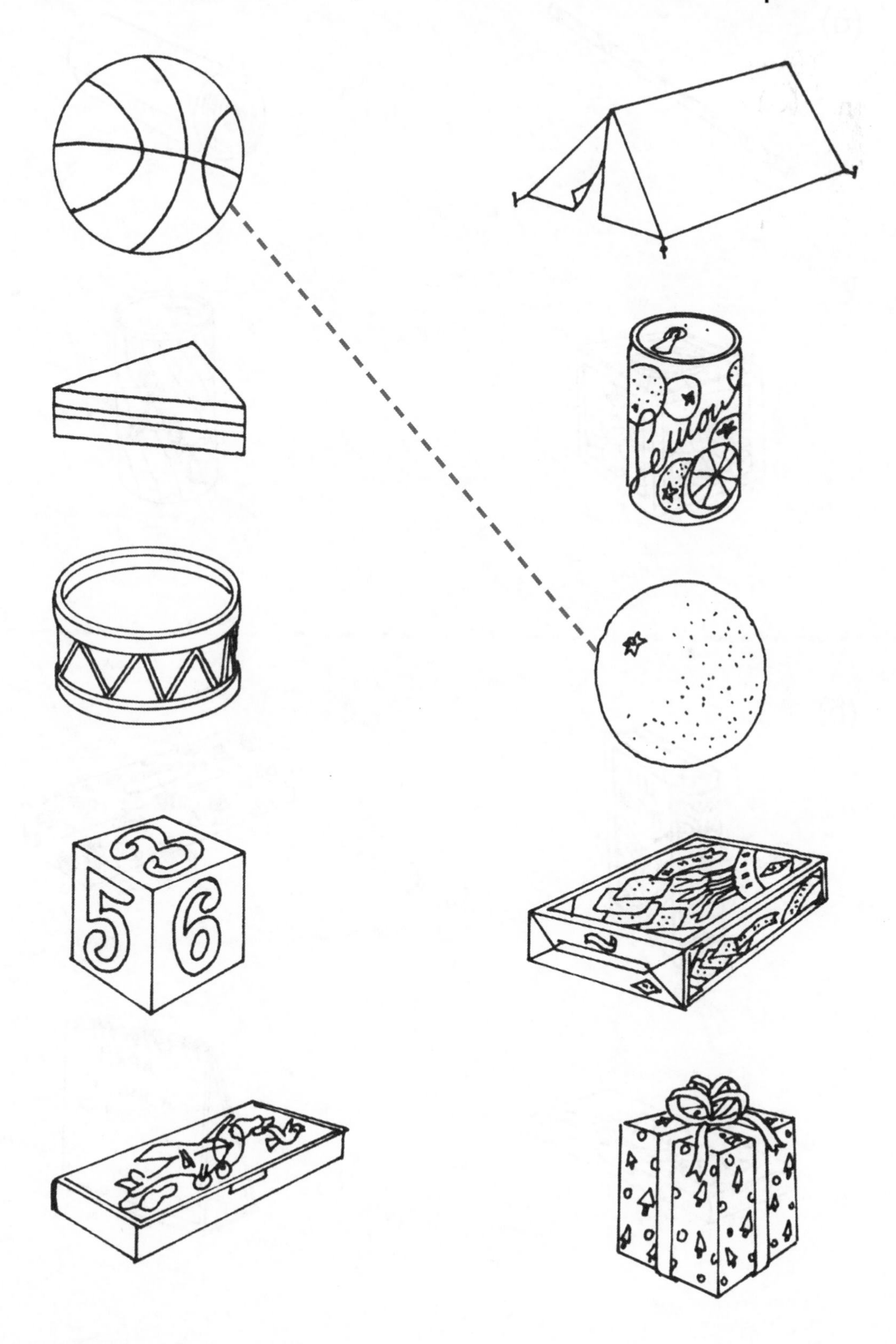

2. Which object has a shape different from the others? Cross (✗) it out.

(a)

(b)

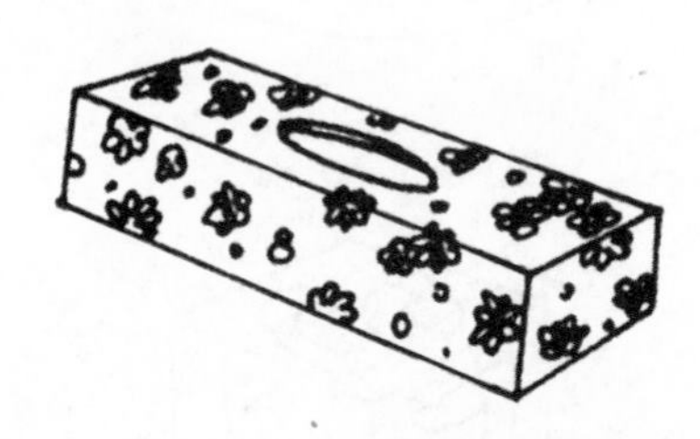

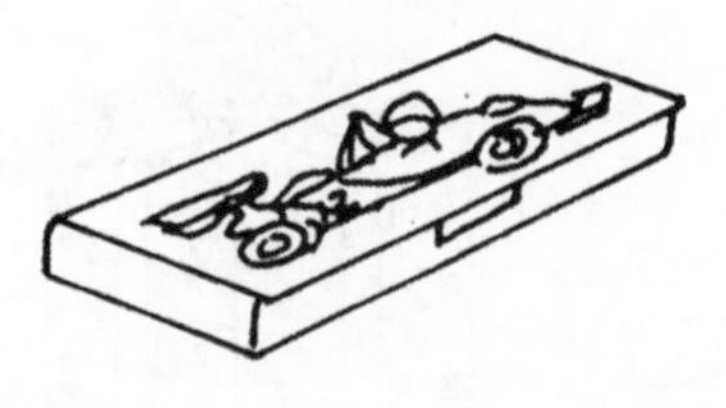

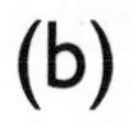

3. Name the shape of the face that is shaded.

(a)

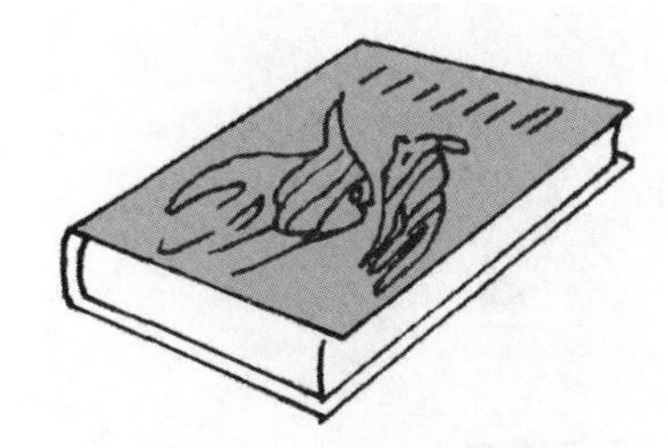

____

(b)

____

(c)

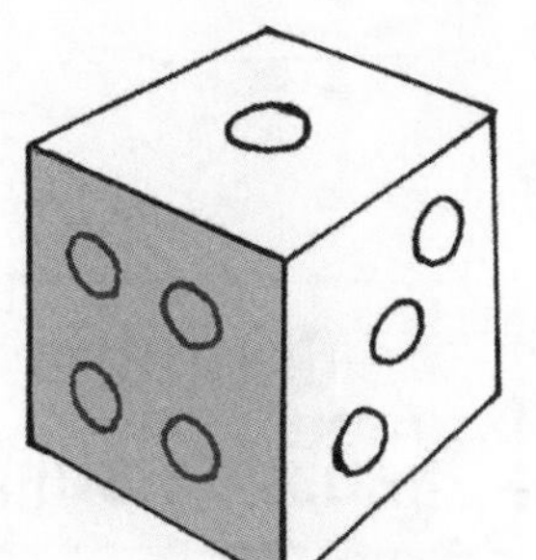

____

(d)

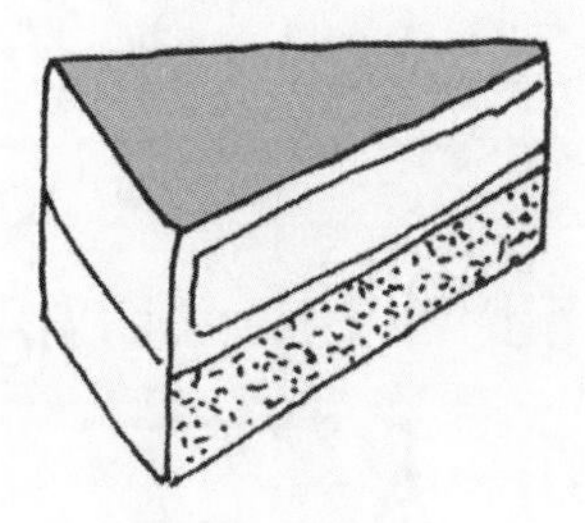

____

(e)

____

(f)

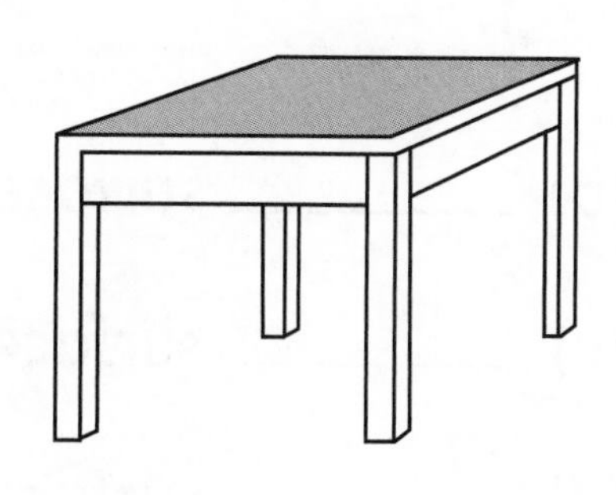

____

4. (a) Count the flat and curved surfaces of each solid. Complete the table below.

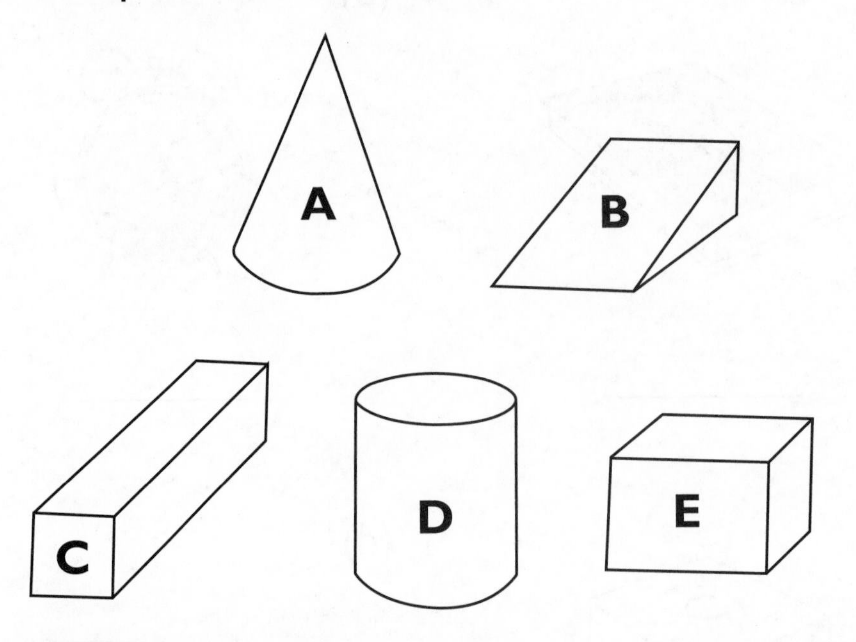

Solid	Number of flat surfaces	Number of curved surfaces
A		
B		
C		
D		
E		

(b) ________ surfaces of Solid B are triangles.

(c) ________ surfaces of Solid C are squares.

(d) ________ surfaces of Solid D are circles.

EXERCISE 2

1. Trace this shape four times on a piece of paper.
   Cut out the pieces.

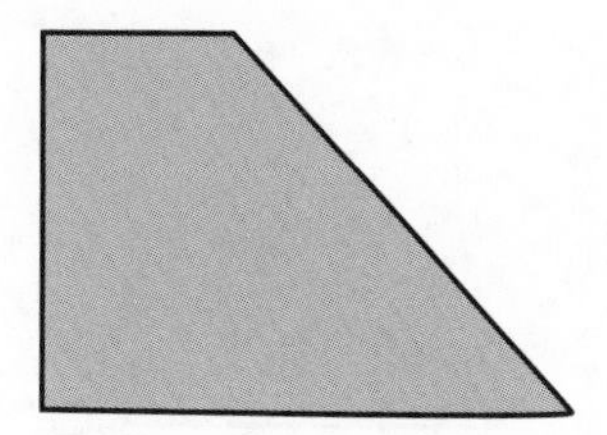

   Use the four pieces to form each of the shapes below.
   Draw dotted lines on each shape to show how
   it is formed. The first one has been done for you.

   (a)

   (b)

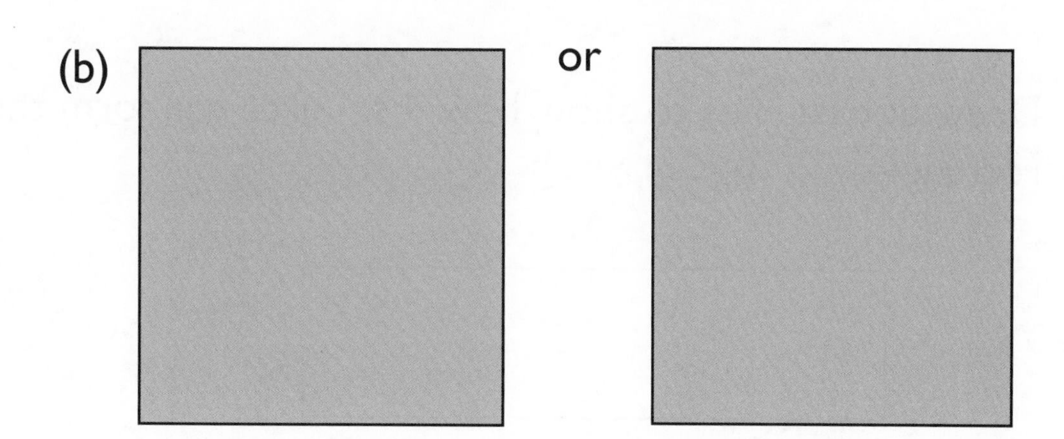

(c)

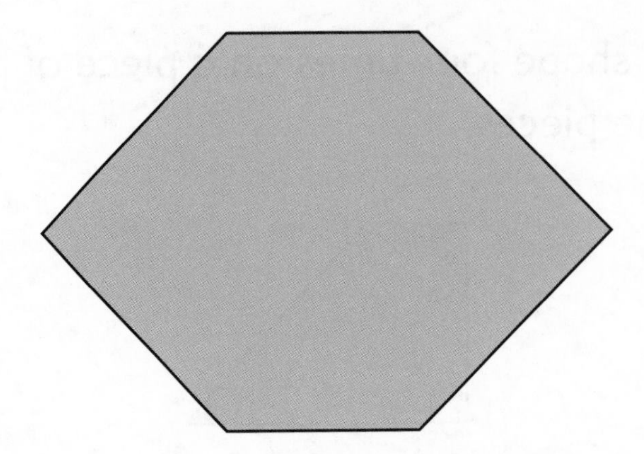

2. Draw dotted lines to show how 8 squares can form the rectangle.

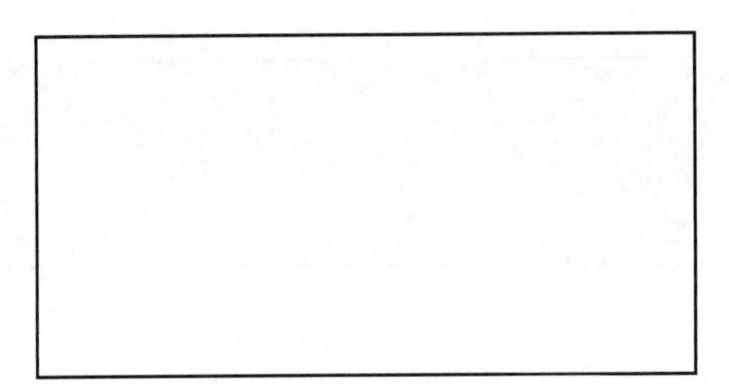

3. Draw dotted lines to show how 4 squares can form the rectangle.

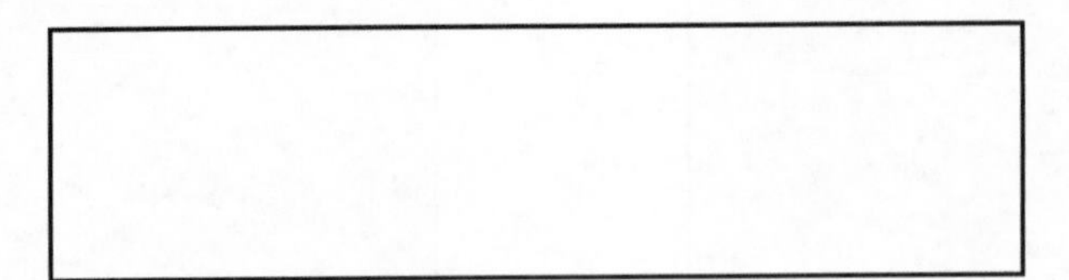

EXERCISE 3

1. This figure is formed by two straight lines and two curves.

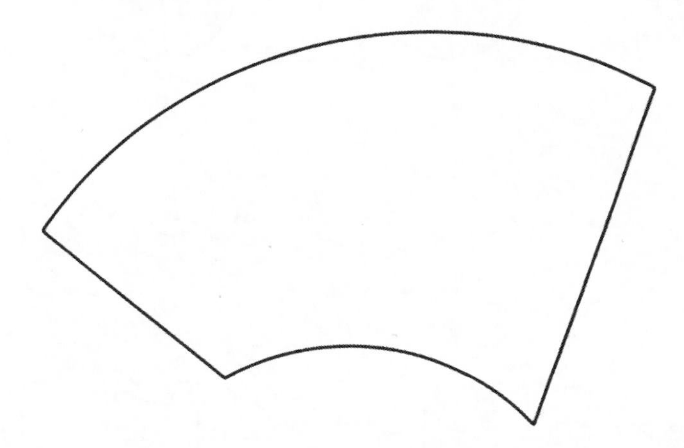

Draw another figure with two straight lines and two curves.

2. Join the two parts that form a circle.

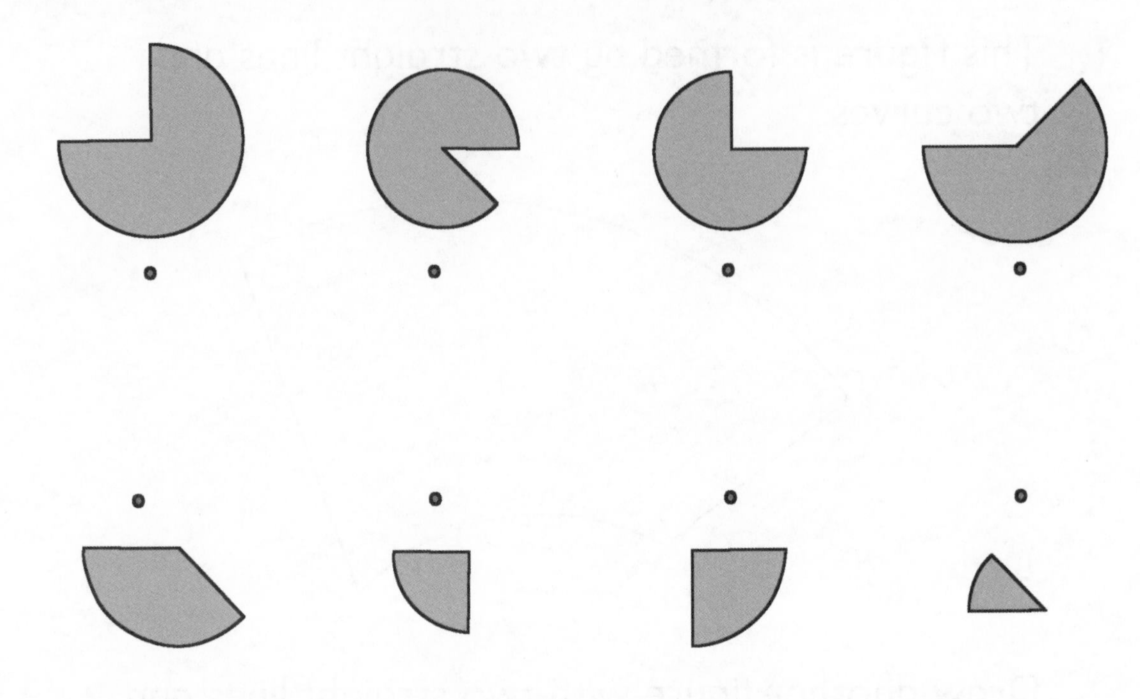

3. Join the two parts that form a square.

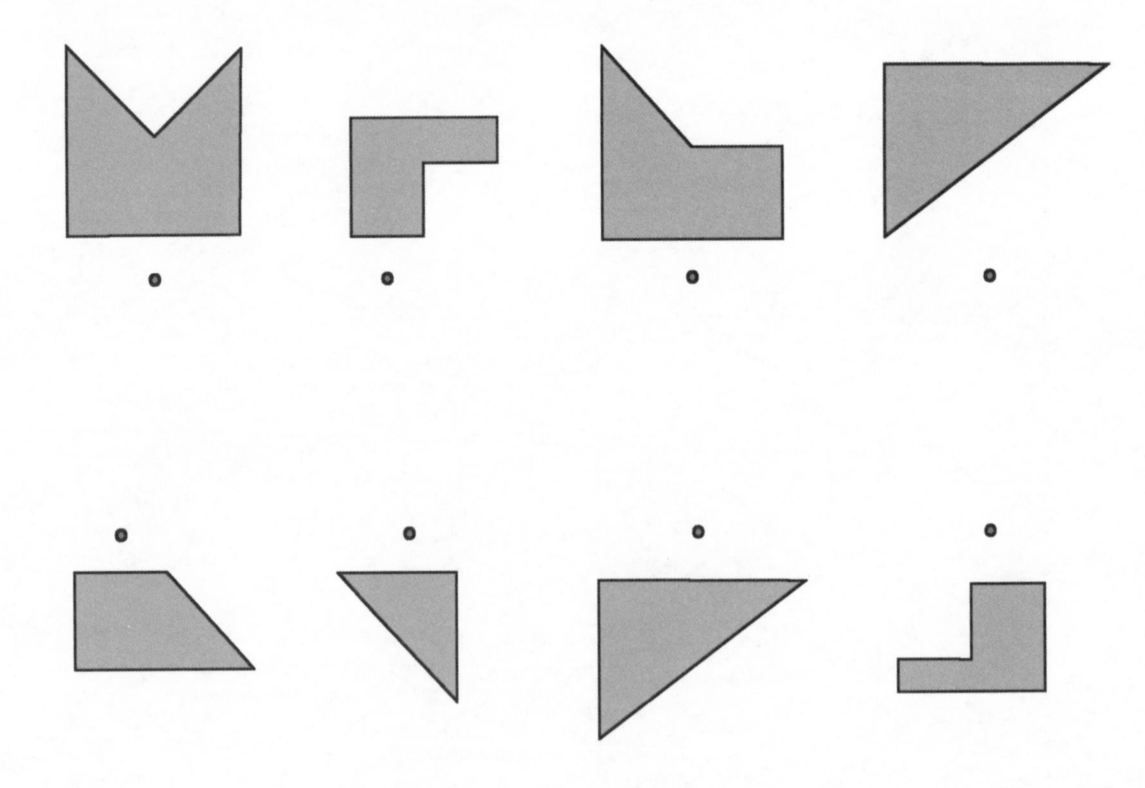

EXERCISE 4

1. 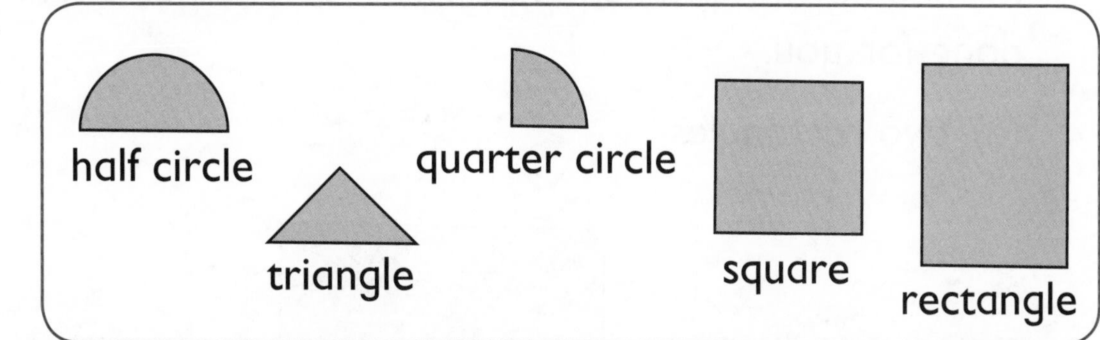

Each of the following figures is made up of two of the above shapes.

Draw a dotted line on each figure to show how it is formed.
Name the two shapes.

(a) 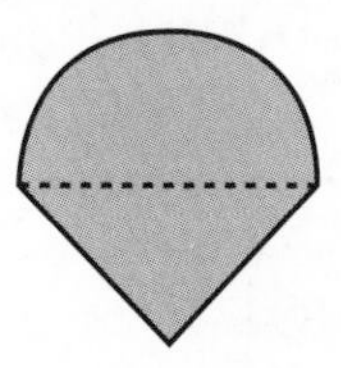

half circle ________

____

(b) 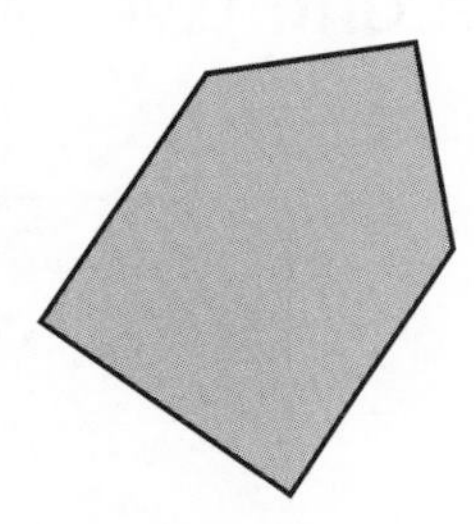

____

____

(c) 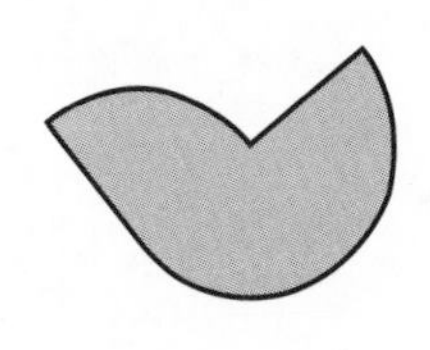

____

____

(d) 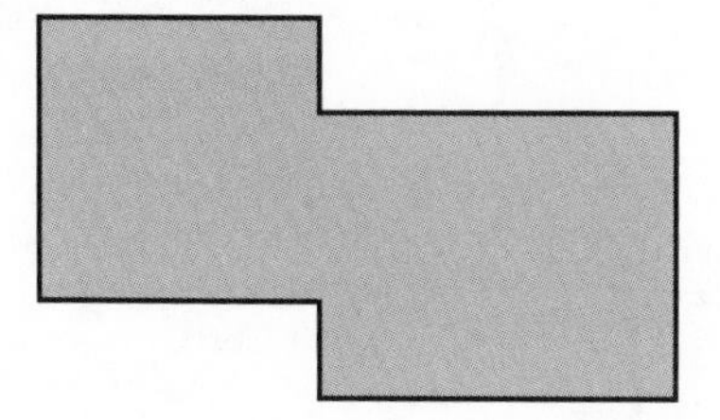

____

____

(e) 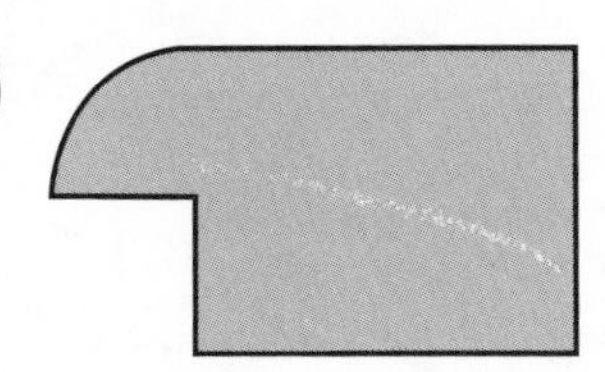

____

____

2. Draw dotted lines on each figure to show how it is formed by the given shapes. The first one has been done for you.

(a) two rectangles

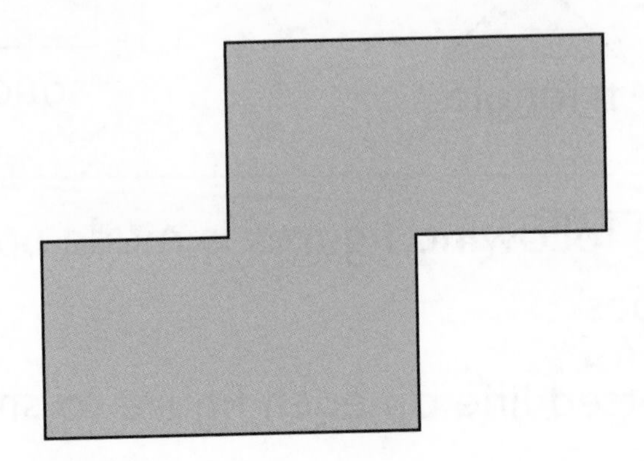

(b) one rectangle and two squares

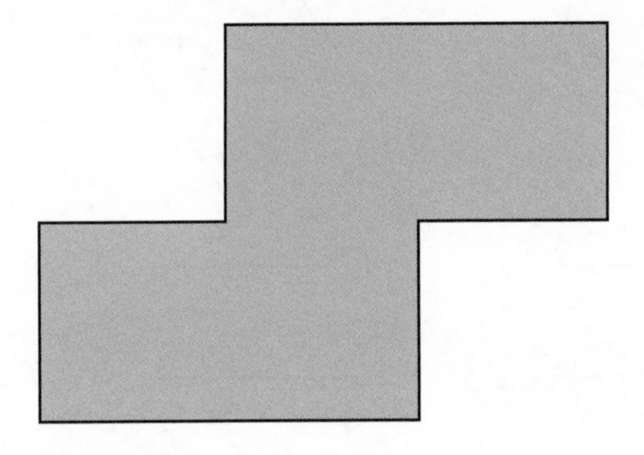

(c) a half circle and a rectangle

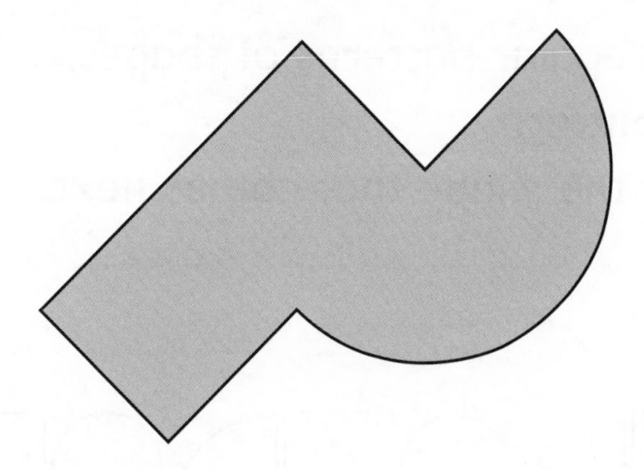

(d) two quarter circles and a square

(e) a rectangle, a triangle, and a half circle

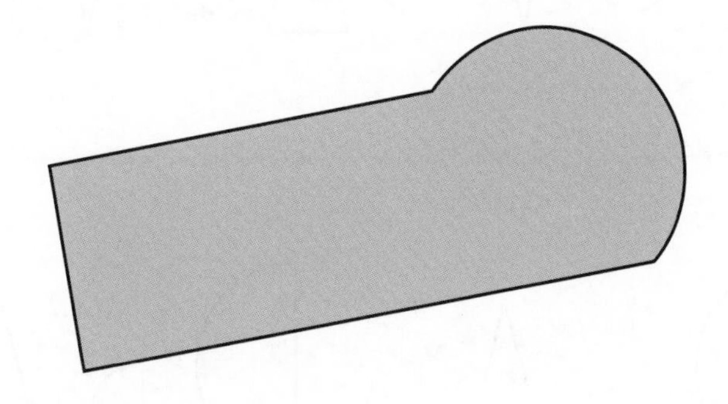

EXERCISE 5

1. These are regular patterns of shapes.
   Find each pattern.
   Then color the shape that comes next.

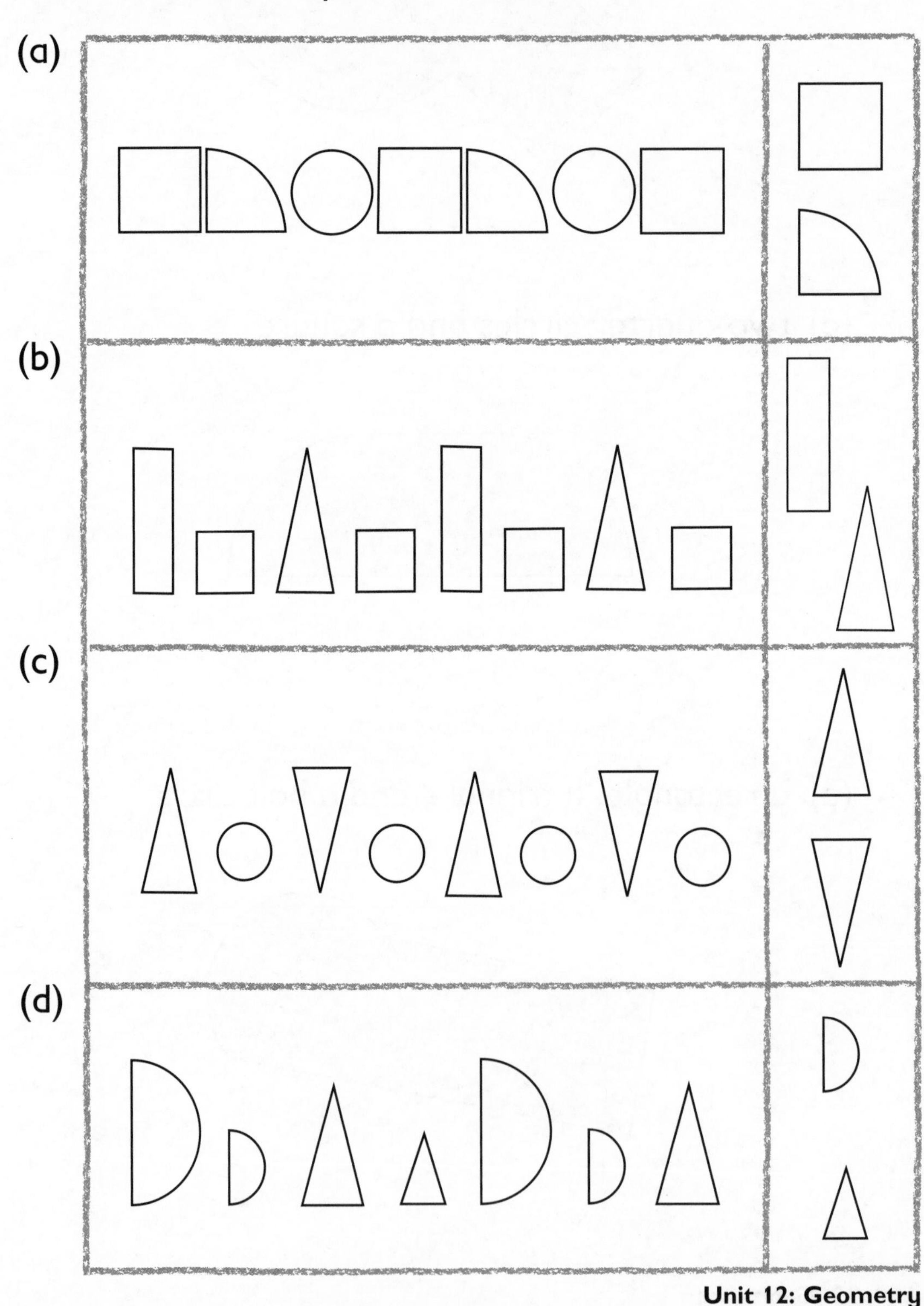

2. Study each regular pattern.
Then draw the shape that completes the pattern.

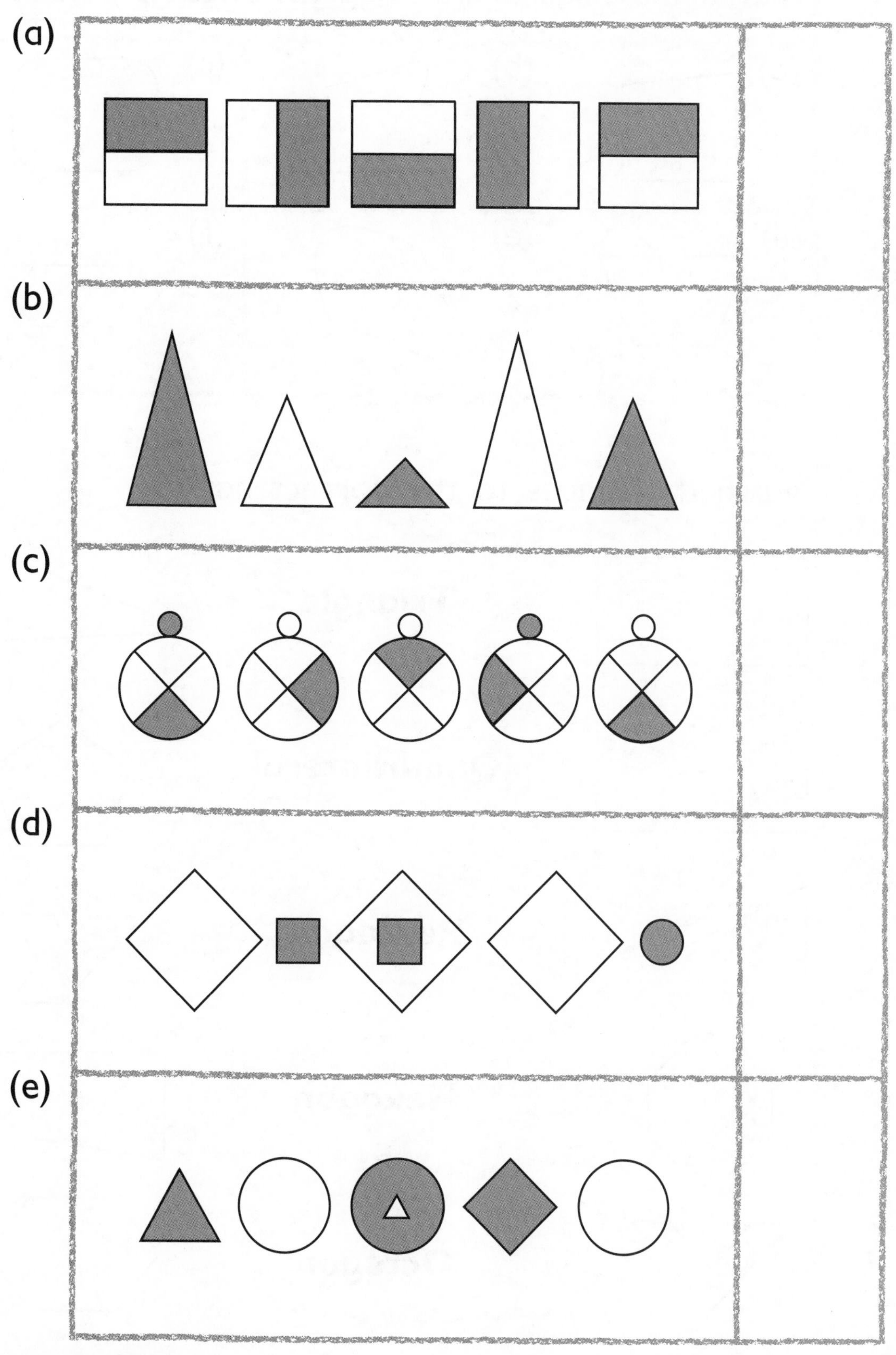

EXERCISE 6

1. Which of these figures are polygons? Check (✓) the boxes.

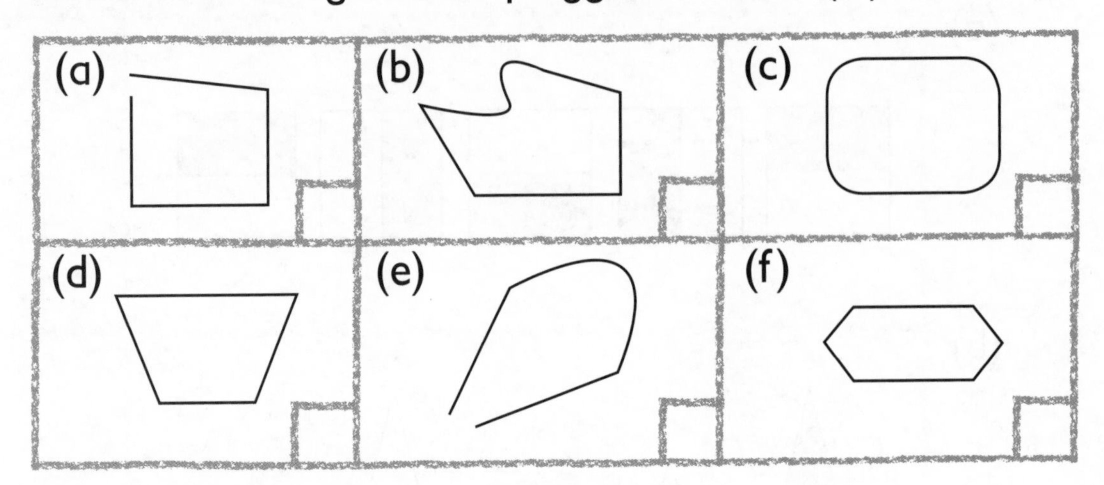

2. Match the shapes to the correct names.

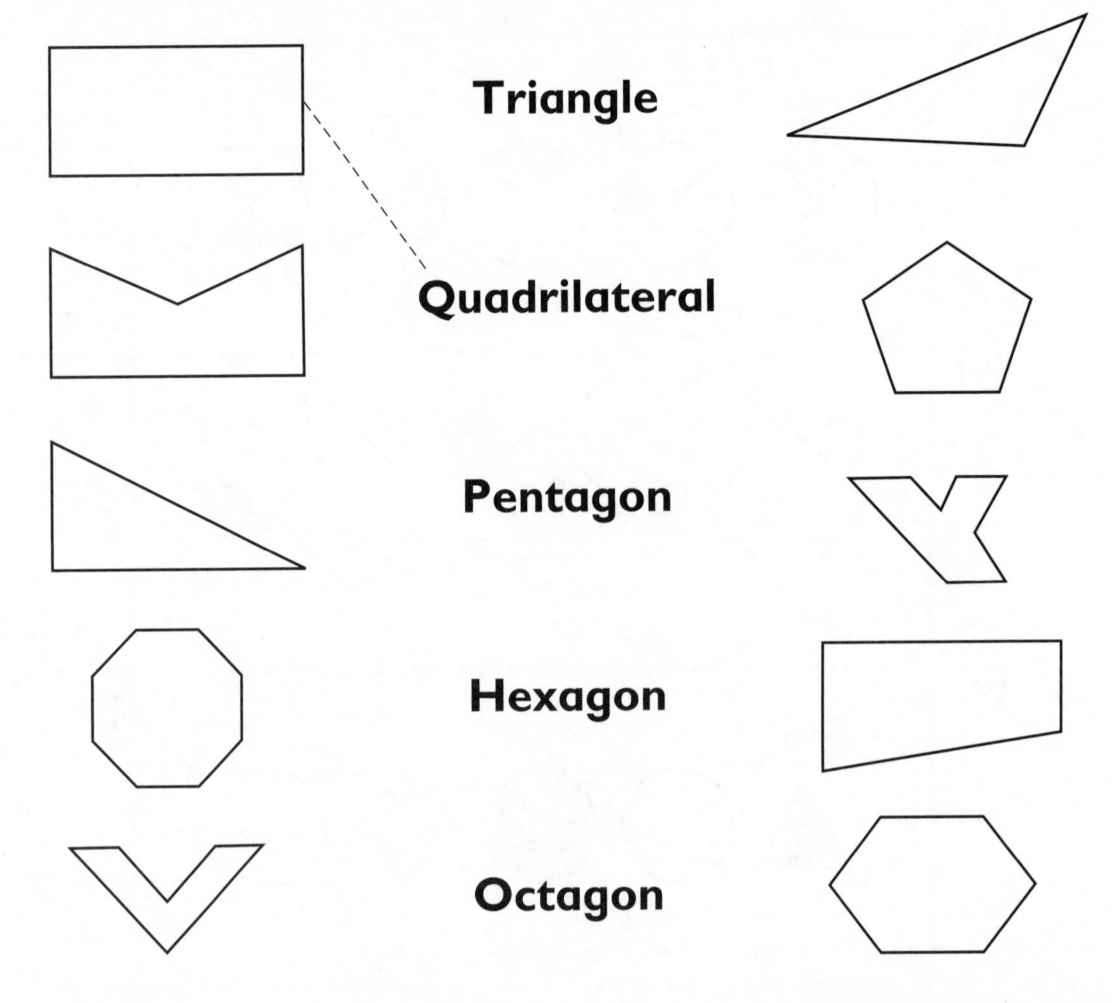

3. Mark the angles of each figure.
Then complete the table below.

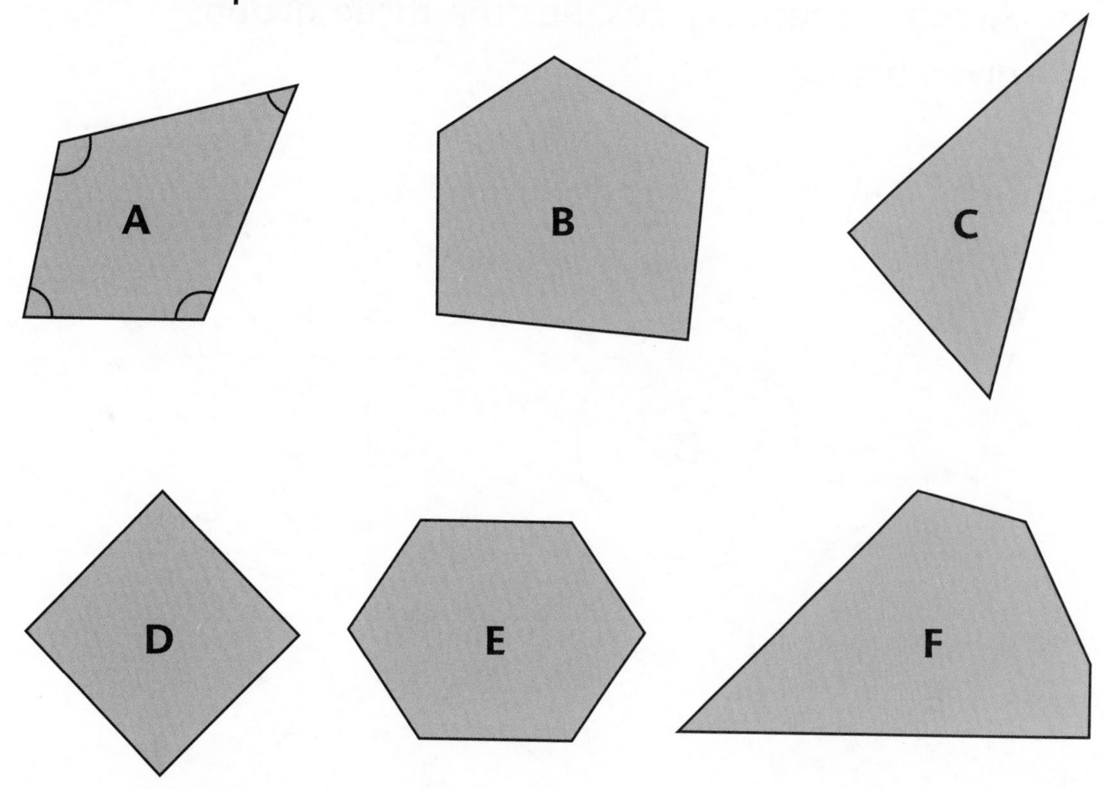

Figure	Number of sides	Number of angles	Name of polygon
A			
B			
C			
D			
E			
F			

REVIEW 12

1. Arrange these figures into the three groups given below.

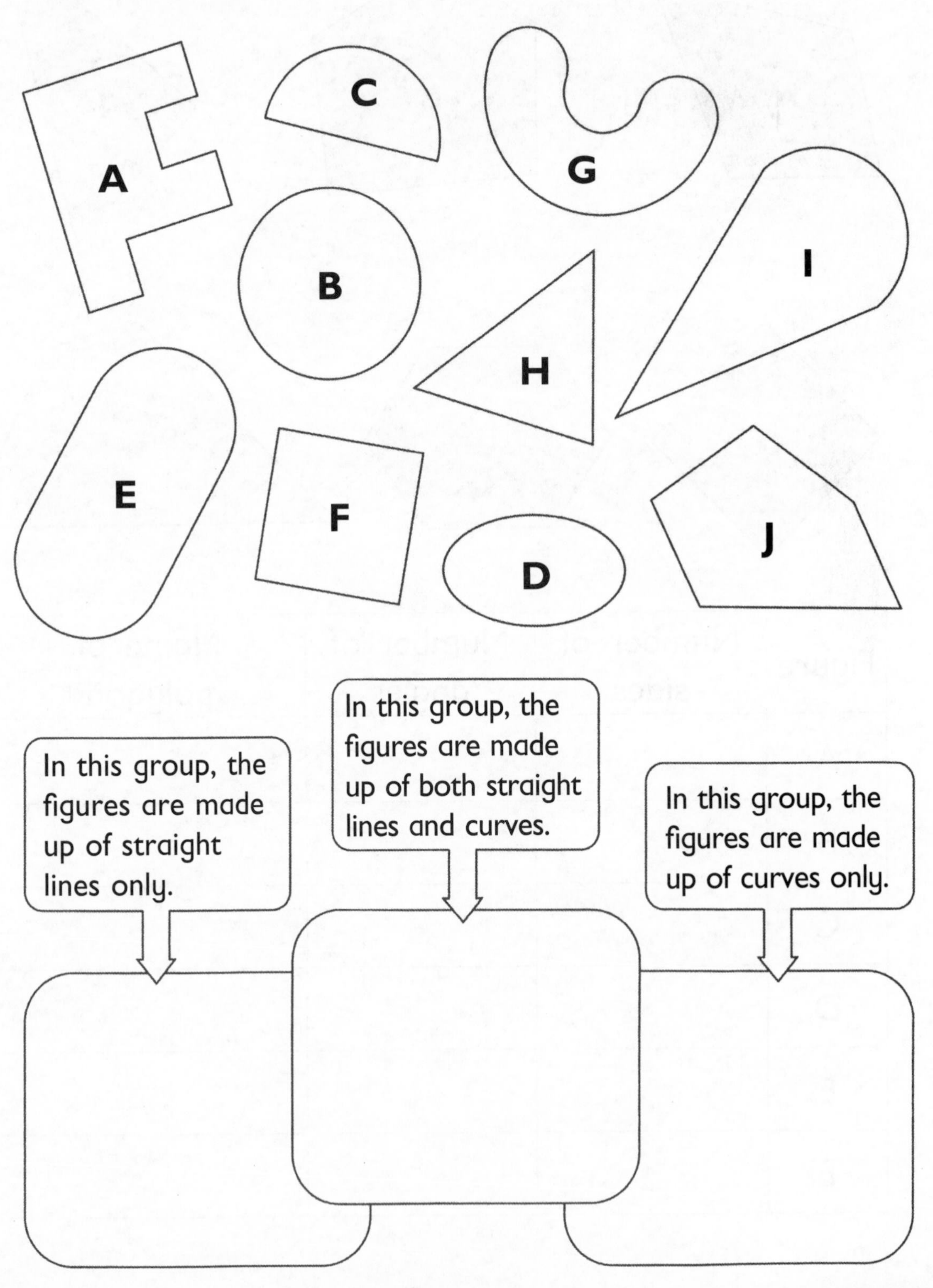

2. Fill in the blanks.

(a) The solid has ________ flat surfaces.

(b) ________ surfaces are rectangles.

3. How many □ do you need to make this rectangle?

____

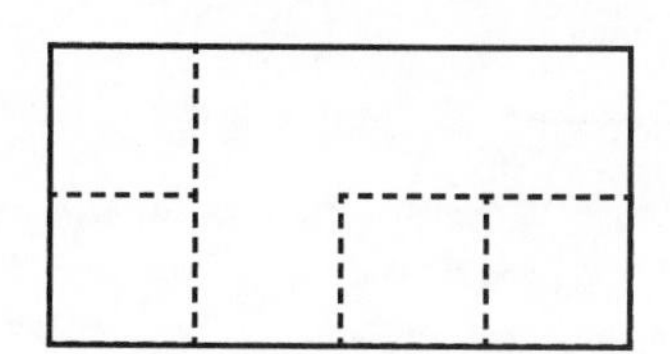

4. Each of the following figures is made up of two shapes.
Draw a dotted line on each figure to show how it is formed and name the two shapes.

(a) 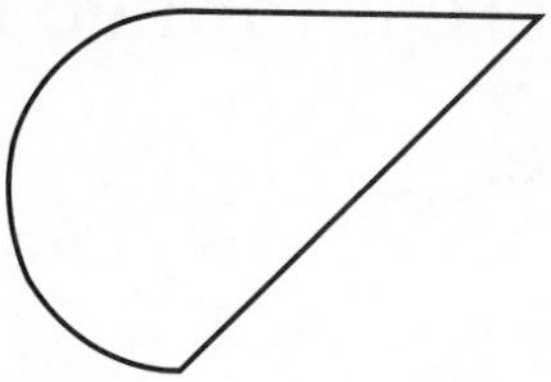 This figure is made up of

a ________ and a ________.

(b) 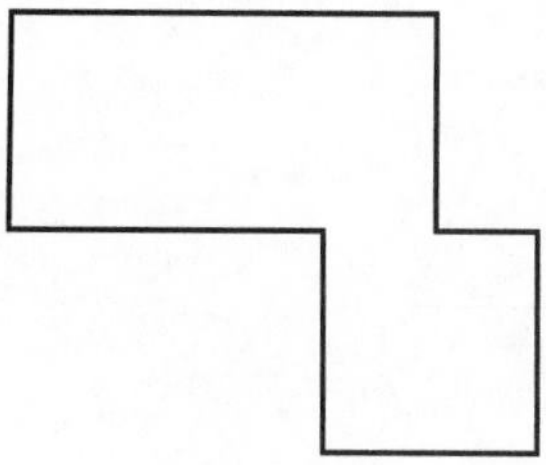 This figure is made up of

a ________ and a ________.

5. Look at the shaded surfaces in the pictures.
Match them to the shapes below.
Write the letter that represents the shape in the blank.

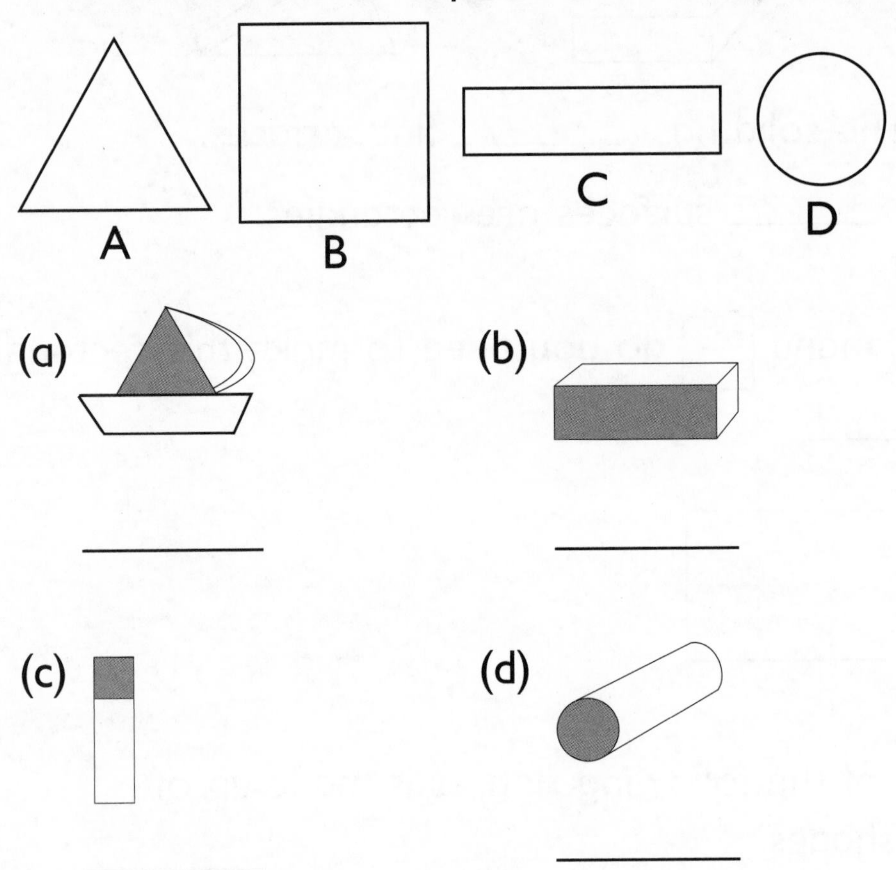

6. Draw 2 lines to show how the figure is formed by a half circle, a triangle, and a square.

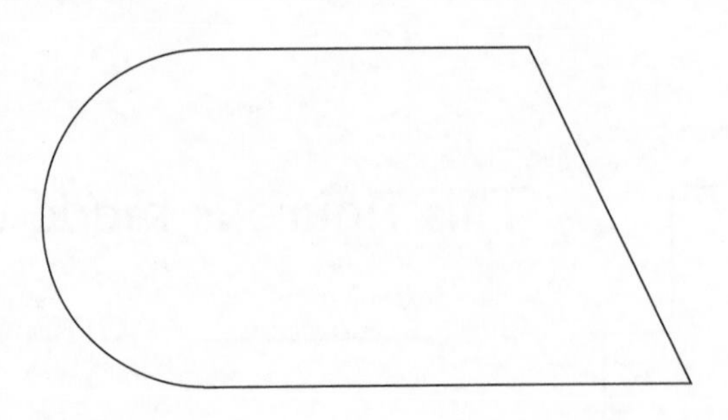

7. Fill in the blanks.

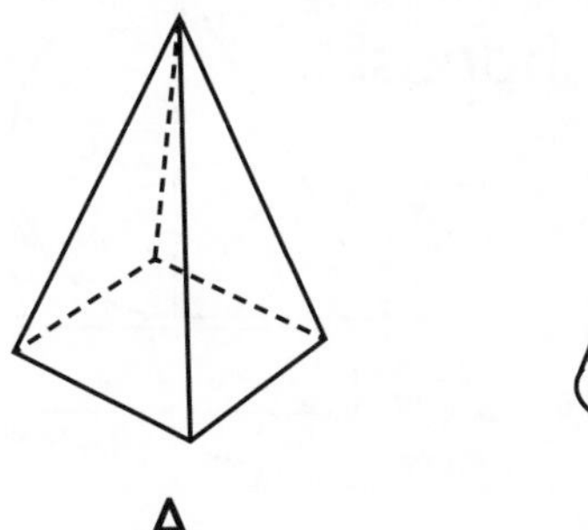
A

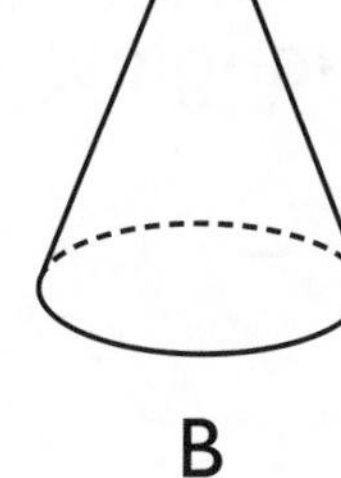
B

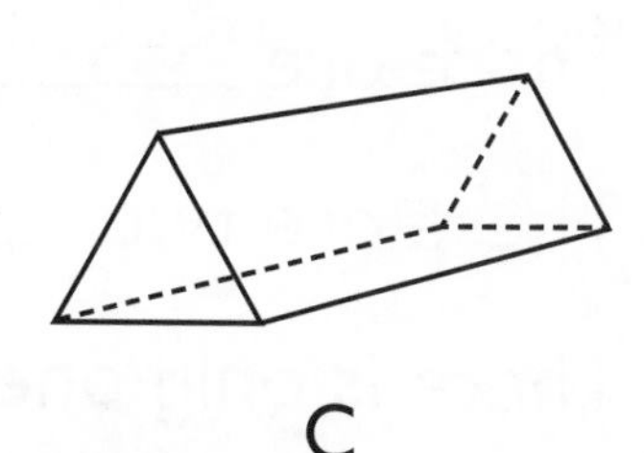
C

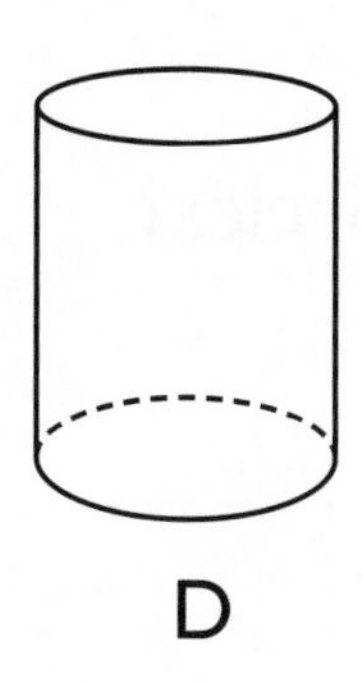
D

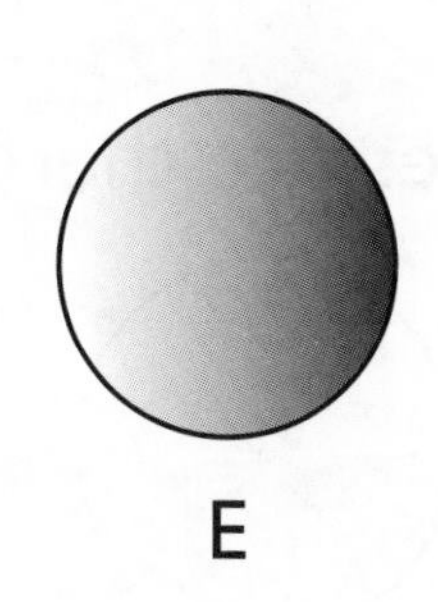
E

(a) __________ and __________ have one curved surface.

(b) __________ has no edges and no flat surfaces.

(c) __________ and __________ have only flat surfaces.

8. Study each regular pattern.

Then draw the correct shape in the space provided.

(a)

(b)

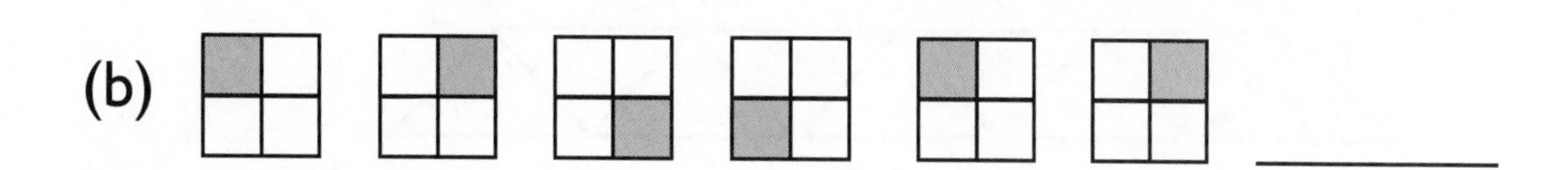

9. Fill in the blanks.

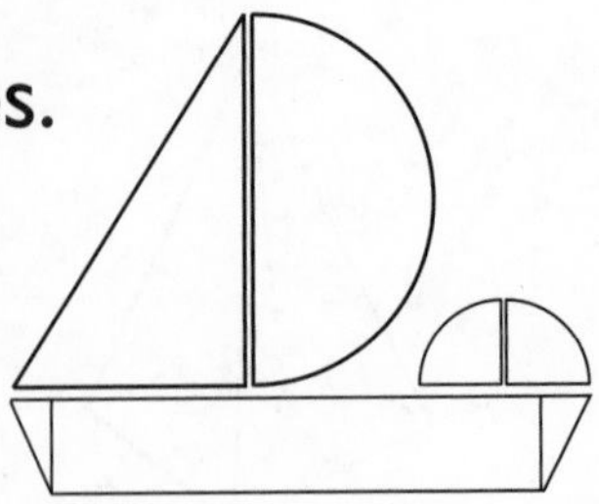

(a) There are ________ different shapes.

(b) There are ________ triangles.

(c) There are two ________.

(d) There is only one ________

and one ________.

10. How many quarter circles are there in 3 circles?

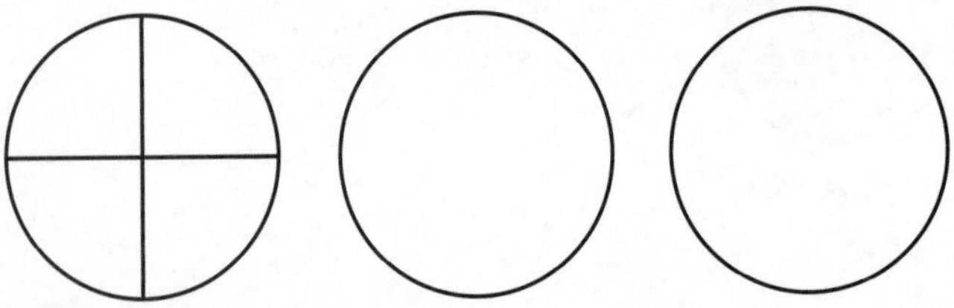

There are ________ quarter circles in 3 circles.

11. Each of the following figures is made up of two different shapes. Name the two shapes.

(a) ________ ________

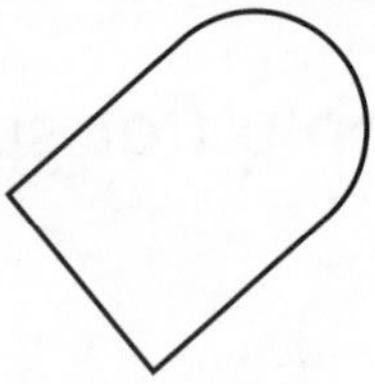

(b) ________ ________

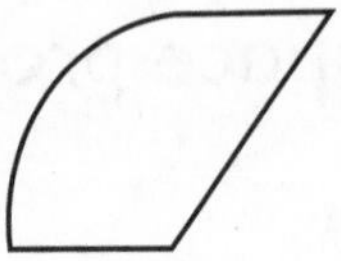

12. How many △ are used to form this shape?

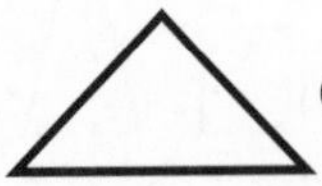

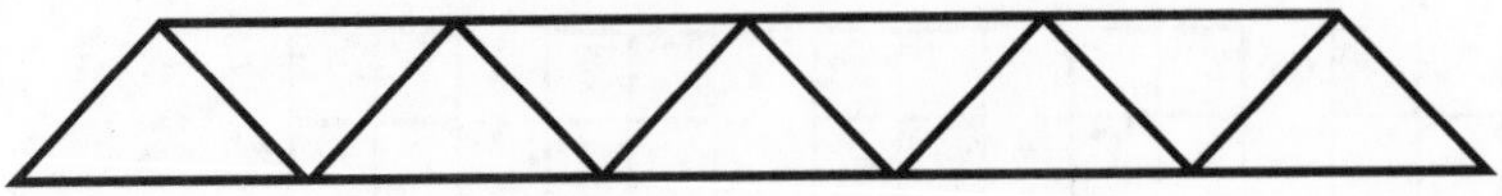

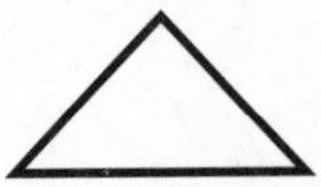

________ △ are used.